Social Evolution

DUCKWORTH DEBATES IN ARCHAEOLOGY
Series editor: Richard Hodges

Also available

Archaeology and Text
John Moreland

Beyond Celts, Germans and Scythians
Peter S. Wells

Debating the Archaeological Heritage
Robin Skeates

Loot, Legitimacy and Ownership
Colin Renfrew

Origins of the English
Catherine Hills

The Roman Countryside
Stephen L. Dyson

Shipwreck Archaeology
Sean Kingsley

State Formation in Early China
Li Liu & Xingcan Chen

Towns and Trade in the Age of Charlemagne
Richard Hodges

Villa to Village
Riccardo Francovich & Richard Hodges

DUCKWORTH DEBATES IN ARCHAEOLOGY

Social Evolution

Mark Pluciennik

Duckworth

First published in 2005 by
Gerald Duckworth & Co. Ltd.
90-93 Cowcross Street, London EC1M 6BF
Tel: 020 7490 7300
Fax: 020 7490 0080
inquiries@duckworth-publishers.co.uk
www.ducknet.co.uk

A catalogue record for this book is available
from the British Library

ISBN 0 7156 3287 6

Typeset by Ray Davies
Printed and bound in Great Britain by
Biddles Ltd, King's Lynn, Norfolk

Contents

For Sarah, Rachel and Adam

Illustrations

Figs 1-3 are reproduced by permission of the Founders' Library, University of Wales, Lampeter.

Introduction

What is social evolution? At its simplest it is a description of the stages through which human societies are said to have passed from their beginnings until the modern world took shape. In its first modern expression by mid-eighteenth-century authors in north-west Europe these stages were said to have been those of savage hunters, barbarian herders, then civilised farmers and finally traders – the Age of Commerce. Since then both our terminologies and to a certain extent our categories have changed. Archaeologists and anthropologists no longer talk of 'savages' and 'barbarians', though we still have specialists in foraging, pastoralist, farming or peasant, and urban societies. In archaeology the palaeolithic and neolithic periods in Eurasia also reflect social evolutionary stages of hunters and farmers respectively, though the history of how they came to do so is not straightforward. It is for this reason that in this book, the term 'social evolution' refers not to the fact of archaeologically and historically recorded changes in the past, but rather to the idea that the archaeological record can be so described.

However, we can see that even expressed in its simplest form social evolution raises questions which go beyond the descriptive. For example, since individuals and societies variably dependent upon hunting, herding, farming and commerce co-exist in the world today, how helpful are such stages when treated as an historical sequence? Are we referring only to certain regions and societies, with all the problems of defining spatial and social continuity which that raises when looking back over five, ten or a hundred thousand years? Can only some of these be said to have evolved? Or is it meant to be a scheme applicable to the whole human race, a general history? If so, what might it mean to be or to describe a member of a society judged to be at a less evolved or earlier historical stage? Are these terms which should be reserved for largely prehistoric peoples and only over the long term and in the broadest syntheses? Why should we use these categories to define some stages and not others? Should we use stadial schemes at all, treat them rather as Weberian ideal types, or adopt some other and perhaps less rigid way of thinking about social change? What is the value of social evolution as a concept? Is it 'the most inane, sterile, and pernicious theory ever conceived in the history of science' (Laufer 1918: 90, cited by White 1959: vii), 'the most challenging and rewarding task any anthropologist can undertake' (Carneiro 2003: 288), or somewhere in between? What do archaeologists think about social evolution today?

Here are two recent views of the matter:

> Probably no other concept has wreaked such damage within the social and historical sciences as the notion of social evolution.
>
> Tilley 1995: 338

> [T]here is at this stage in human history a strong need to believe in the possibility of being able to create a future that is better than the present. ... the concept of sociocultural evolution has been progressively refined since the eighteenth century and is now better suited than ever before to play such a role.
>
> Trigger 1998: xii

Why should the idea of social evolution raise such passionate and diametrically opposed views? Surely, both members of the public and professional archaeologists might argue, the basic outlines of human history over the last tens or even hundreds of thousands of years are uncontested, and undeniably show change or development – many would say progress – from small groups of foragers living by gathering and hunting, through to villages and cities supported by farming, to complex states, empires and eventually our present world of globally inter-dependent trading states and other entities and institutions. What is there to argue about except the empirical details and perhaps the exact mechanisms involved?

One way to approach the debates about social evolution is to note that while the contents of the term can be taken as a simple description, it has also been a shorthand for other concepts. Social evolution can encompass and be used as a proxy for, or to explain and justify, existing hierarchies, often through now objectionable categories such as race. It has been used as a framework for judging other people and ourselves in a variety of historical and political contexts, and as a view about the shape of human history and our ability, or duty, to control it. Who comprises the 'we' in this instance is also often heavily loaded: typically those writing about social evolution have been those who explicitly or implicitly saw themselves as belonging to societies at the forefront of change in a positive sense; the most advanced, those at the pinnacle of history, looking down or back at other societies, cultures or races. What many of the debates about social evolution centre on, then, is the difficulty of separating fact from value. Social evolution is above all a particular narrative which says much about the holder's or opposer's world view and incorporates deeply held convictions about the nature and meaning of human history, and by impli-cation, about human capacities. Further complications arise because in the light of criticism social evolution has been used as a synonym for 'social change'.

Another reason for revisiting social evolution is simply its longevity as an idea. Although of course we have much more empirical detail and different philosophical and theoretical traditions available to us today, social evolution in outline has remained a foundation for long-term histories since its classical expositions more than two hundred and fifty years ago. When so much else has changed, in theory and method, political context and socio-cultural mores over that time, we should at least ask why the idea has persisted. One answer could be that what we mean by social evolution is simply not the same as it was for earlier writers. Another might be that it is simply true, in the same way that we would accept that the earth is round and orbits the sun: but I shall argue that even the simplest categories and terms that we might choose to describe *any* outline of social evolution are the product of a particular mind-set and historical circumstances, and inevitably raise other issues, as well as possibilities for other histories.

Partly because of its long history, social evolution, unlike many more specialised concepts such as ritual or stratigraphy, has had a prominent public life too. It pre-existed archaeology and sociology (and the theory of biological evolution), and was introduced within genres which were little to do with archaeology as we would define it today. A lay version of social evolution still informs many public attitudes towards history and other peoples, and influences governmental foreign policies, for example. The idea of progress, one of the key ideological tenets of the western* world since the eighteenth century, is closely related to social evolution, as are other attitudes such as orientalism (Said 1978). It is often, then, one of the unquestioned western or modern 'truths' which from our point of view is difficult to stand back from and to question, but which underlies many current perceptions, stereotypes, policies and

---

*'Western' is in itself a problematic term. Here I want to use it to refer to ideas or policies originally emanating from Europe or European-dominated or influenced cultures (such as America), as opposed to Asian or African philosophies of history, for example.

14

actions in the past and present. For example, in Britain the distinguished military historian Sir John Keegan recently wrote:

> This war [against terrorism] belongs within the much larger spectrum of a far older conflict between settled, creative productive Westerners and predatory, destructive Orientals.
>
> It is no good pretending that the peoples of the desert and the empty spaces exist on the same level of civilisation as those who farm and manufacture. They do not.
>
> Keegan 2001

However, social evolution is of particular importance for archaeologists and anthropologists because it has been the major force in shaping those disciplines: if we want to understand why certain questions and approaches have been dominant, then we must consider the history and ramifications of the concept. For example, many of the 'big' questions of origin and transition in (pre)history and archaeology are predicated upon a certain view of the past which often derives directly from the stages defined by social evolution. Thus the transition from forager to farmer and the origins of agriculture have in part attracted so much attention because they represent what are seen as massive discontinuities – revolutions – which need to be explained in particular ways. There are, of course, as for any period and place, interesting questions to be asked about archaeologically observable changes and what they meant and mean. But one reason why we focus on particular aspects, times and places is because a social evolutionary framework sets up conceptual boundaries between certain types of society. Thus much effort has been expended upon what was earlier called 'the rise of civilisation' – the origin of states, especially in south-west Asia – which again can be argued to have diverted effort from different historical trajectories in other places (such as Africa: see Keech McIntosh 1999). Others have argued that

15

pervading notions of what constitutes the rise of 'social complexity' have emphasised only certain societies which are traditionally seen as direct ancestors of modern European or other western polities (Chapman 2003: 164-86).

Although trends related to many other intellectual, cultural and socio-political currents influence what we study and how, it remains the fact that in anthropology and archaeology there are major contemporary divides among those who research and teach about hunter-gatherers, those who study peasant societies and those who focus on urban or state societies. Certainly in archaeological terms there appears to be no necessary reason why the human past has to be divided up in this particular way. There are more subtle effects too: for example, studies of the lithic component of the archaeological record may be downgraded or even ignored as soon as pottery is present. This may be partly for empirical reasons, since pottery can be more abundant and demonstrate greater stylistic variety; but equally it may implicitly be valued more highly, as a signifier of progress, civilisation and farming societies, and be thus deemed worthy of more archaeological attention.

Social evolution, then, as a philosophy and an intellectual framework impinges upon archaeology and anthropology at many levels, and has had many consequences beyond the purely academic and intellectual worlds. Categories and themes deriving from social evolution still structure much current research. As one of the most persistent meta-narratives in western thought, it has had a profound impact on government policies and on many aspects of relations of the west with other parts of the world. Rooted in attitudes articulated within the early capitalism of northern Europe, it lay at the heart of colonialism and imperialism, and is intimately associated with racism. However, since the meaning and contexts of the concept have not remained unchanged over the two hundred and fifty years of its existence, this book adopts both an historical and a

Introduction

comparative approach to the topic. While discussing the sources, transformations and implications of social evolutionary views, it also points to alternative conceptualisations of human history. It asks whether it is possible and desirable to disentangle ideas of social evolution and of progress from judgements about the relative value of ways of being, of forms of social and economic complexity, and of what the archaeological and historical records tell us about the course of human history.

I need to emphasise that this book is not meant as a discussion of the substantive or methodological contents of social evolution – about how we should do it – nor as a general review. This is partly for reasons of space; and also because there are very many excellent books which offer positive or critical perspectives from a variety of disciplinary positions (e.g. Harris 1979, 2001; Rindos 1984; Boyd & Richerson 1985; Ingold 1986; Johnson & Earle 1987, 2000; Hallpike 1988; Sanderson 1995; Trigger 1998; Shennan 2002; Carneiro 2003). It is rather meant as reflection on the role which the concept of social evolution has played within the historical disciplines, primarily archaeology and anthropology, and the underlying sources, themes and implications. Finally I should explain my own biases, in case they do not become apparent throughout the book: I began pondering many of these issues fifteen years ago during my doctoral research into the Mesolithic-Neolithic transition in the central Mediterranean. For the obsession with the distinctions made between foragers and farmers, I can only apologise. I have often felt frustrated at the ways that research into these periods is so heavily structured by existing traditions of thought, yet criticism seems mostly to enable reproduction of those same categories. I have not yet found a satisfactory solution, but clarifying some of the issues may help suggest other ways of writing histories.

1

The sources of social evolution

Writing the history of an idea often leads to a search for the first occurrence which can be used to ascribe responsibility to a particular author or thinker: a kind of original sin or stroke of genius depending on one's viewpoint. More valuable are social histories of ideas which examine broad shifts in sensibility or circumstances that enable particular ideas and terminologies to gain currency in ways which resonate with other concerns and values of the time. Nevertheless as exemplars one can point at two individuals in north-west Europe who expressed similar ideas about social evolution in similar terms at around the same time: the economist Adam Smith, lecturing in Scotland, and the French thinker Turgot, whose *Universal History* remained an unpublished manuscript for many years. Both presented a version of stadial social evolution around the middle of the eighteenth century, in which they described a sequence from savage hunters, to barbarian herders, followed by civilised farmers and finally what Adam Smith called the Age of Commerce – his contemporary times. Within a decade there were many other books which followed or repeated the same scheme, and for the second half of the eighteenth century, the peak of the Age of Enlightenment, many, if not most, of the writers who dealt with such matters accepted this outline of a general, or 'conjectural' human history.

Most of the volumes in which these histories appeared did

not and could not, given the lack of any systematic archaeology, examine prehistory as a matter of interest in itself: rather they were exploring ideas of law, property, trade and economic relations, and political organisation, rights such as those over natives and their land in colonies, and religious and moral duties. These conjectural histories were usually short preambles to the main topic of interest and later, in the nineteenth century especially, would become formulaic. There were some books, however, such as Robertson's 1777 *History of America*, which were more anthropological in content, and which made continual reference to such schemes insofar as they described reported practices of indigenous peoples to show how earlier 'primitives' or 'savages' may have behaved.

There is a series of questions which this phenomenon invites: why was it at this particular time, around 1750, that these schemata first appeared? Is there any significance in the fact that it was in north-west Europe? Why did they become so readily accepted, at least among the intelligentsia? Why did they appear in this particular form, using subsistence as the primary category? Can we see precursors, or was it really a radically new idea? To answer these kinds of questions convincingly would require a knowledge of European cultural, social and economic histories of the seventeenth and eighteenth centuries far beyond any which I would claim. Nevertheless, there are hints which may at least point us in the right direction. But first of all, one has to deal with the issue of whether there really is a new phenomenon to be explained: what did previous writers say about the outline of human history?

The idea of progress in human history and the related concept of improvement has been recognised by historians as one which is particularly associated with modern times, that is, the last three centuries, and with the west. There were and are other ways of viewing the past which will be considered later. While progress can be considered as a modern ideology, it is not

1. The sources of social evolution

an idea without precedent. Some, such as Nisbet (1980), have therefore sought to identify its earliest occurrence or to trace continuity into modern times. It is true to say that one can find Classical writers such as Lucretius or Hesiod in which change, largely for the better, characterises their schematic views of the past. But by and large, such progressive histories are not a concern: where cultural difference or what we might now call alterity or 'Otherness' is the topic, it is not necessarily arranged developmentally (McGrane 1989; Janko 1997). By medieval times in Europe, it can be argued that Christian understandings of the meaning of history, derived from the Bible, predominate. Although one can interpret the Bible in various ways, the story of human expulsion from the Garden of Eden invited the view that history since that time has been one of degeneration or stagnation, even if there will eventually be salvation of a spiritual, rather than material nature, whether individually or collectively.

If this reading is correct, what is it then that had changed by the mid-eighteenth century to enable progressive stadial schemes to be so rapidly accepted by the intelligentsia? For the economic historian Ronald Meek (1976: 127), social evolution arose where, when and in the form that it did because of rapid observable economic change and the resultant contrast 'between areas which are economically advancing and areas which are still in "lower" stages of development'. These material conditions undoubtedly played a part, but to explain social evolution in this way seems to beg the question. We need to consider a series of trends and changes in intellectual as well as material circumstances which led thinkers to confront and analyse their own world from a different perspective. These factors included the 'discovery' of the Americas and their inhabitants, recognition of the importance of trade and profit, often based upon agricultural products, changing attitudes towards the Bible, and a new emphasis on individuality and the duty of people to improve themselves, whether in religious terms aiming towards salvation, or in material terms. This latter aim can be seen as justification for the rising class of merchant capitalists and craftsmen, and led to associated explorations of political theory – how relations between people were ordered. There was a growing acceptance in many spheres of life that one's position and status were not just a matter of birth or (God-given) fate, but also depended upon one's actions and efforts. One way in which these endeavours was recognised was through material success. Some of these changes were matters of concern at the time – Adam Smith's lectures and later publications, including the famous *Wealth of Nations* in 1776, were precisely an exploration and foundation of what we would now call the science of economics. Others are perhaps more easily identified with hindsight as part of long-term shifts in conditions and sensibilities.

What had changed over the years preceding the mid-eighteenth century can be summarised as, firstly, a shift in which relations between people were increasingly being economically, rather than purely socially, defined (Dumont 1977; Appleby 1978). Secondly, there was a growing recognition of the importance of trade and commerce to the relative wealth of nations. The tendency in northern Europe was to ascribe this less to the possession of certain commodities, such as gold, and more to the hard work of the nations involved. One important early contribution to this debate was Mandeville's (1970) *Fable of the Bees* published in 1724. A favourite example was that of the Netherlands, whose commercial wealth and power was admired despite, it was noticed, its small size and lack of native resources. By contrast, it was argued, peoples who lived in naturally abundant countries such as North America but had failed to exploit them, must be lazy or be inherently incapable of using them properly (Fig. 1). This was often used as a justification for colonial settlement. Thus William Robertson

Fig. 1. Native Americans farming in the indigenous manner. An engraving from Pere Lafitau (1724) *Moeurs des Sauvages Ameriquains, comparees aux moeurs des premiers temps,* 2 tomes, Paris: Sangrain & Charles Estienne Hochereau.

(1783, 2: 14) wrote that 'The European colonies have cleared and cultivated a few spots along the coast, but the original inhabitants, as rude and indolent as ever, have done nothing to open or improve a country, possessing almost every advantage of situation or climate'. Later on he asserted that 'As long as hunting continues to be the chief employment of man to which he trusts for subsistence, he can hardly be said to have occupied the earth' (1783, 2: 113). Many similar statements can be found in writers from the later seventeenth century onwards (Pluciennik 2002: 100-9).

Thirdly, from the point of view of Europeans there had been the discovery of new realms of human and geographical difference, primarily in the Americas, which lay outside Biblical and Classical terms of reference and needed somehow to be incorporated into explanations of the world and its history. Fourthly, there was the growth of individualism in the religious, political, philosophical and economic spheres, which placed more emphasis on the duties of people *qua* individuals and their rights to proper rewards for their efforts. However, as a consequence, this also enabled condemnation of those who were deemed unsuccessful. The 'feckless poor', whether at home or abroad, were now often described in these terms, and their failures ascribed to their individual or collective deficiencies as a result of what I have called elsewhere this 'moralisation of labour'. Subsequently, in the nineteenth century, these differences in achievement would often be explained in terms of alleged racial characteristics. Fifthly, there was the growth of Reason – the use of scientific methods to explain, explore and engage with the world. Much of this activity was directed towards agriculture under the name of improvement, 'the application of reason to the soil' (Schaffer 1997), and insistence on the benefits of agricultural enclosure, for example (Fig. 2).

The ubiquity of social evolution thus arose as a culmination of trends, many of which were apparent from at least the

1. The sources of social evolution

Fig. 2. 'Proper' agropastoral farming with ploughs and enclosed fields: note the sheep within the goddess's veil. Engraving from James Thomson's *The Seasons* (1747) by F. Bartolozzi after paintings by W. Hamilton, and published in London by P.W. Tomkins. By contrast, those who objected to enclosure and agricultural improvement would only force us to 'return to our primitive barbarity', according to the Rev. Hewlett, approvingly cited in Arthur Young's 1808 *General Report on Enclosures*.

seventeenth century. Clearly we could trace some of these back further. So although we could propose that social evolution started in 1750 (or 1748, or 1751), this would present precisely the problems characteristic of stadial schemes – they may be useful starting points, but they are always tools, rather than facts. Although with a different emphasis, the anthropologist Alan Barnard (1999, 2004) has examined the eighteenth-century emergence of ideas of hunter-gatherer society. He notes that earlier concerns are rather with distinguishing natural man from civilised man. 'Questions concerning what is innate (individualism or sociality) dominated social thought during the seventeenth century. Mode of subsistence counted for little' (1999: 375). However, the point I wish to emphasise here is that social evolution arose as part of, and in response to, colonial endeavours and incipient capitalism in a particular place and at a particular time. This should alert us to the fact that social evolution is not, or not only, a question of collected empirical observations, but as much an interpretation or an ideology, a culturally and historically contingent attitude towards history and other societies.

To make my position clear, it should be noted that there were also considerable plusses to these Enlightenment views of social evolution and its related philosophies: such conjectural histories assumed the 'unity of mankind' – that physically and psychologically humans were of equal capacity. Consequently rational inquiry could teach us about the natural world, about human institutions such as law and economies, and help us overcome deficiencies in agricultural practices, for example; enable individuals to aspire to conditions and statuses beyond those into which they were born; and ultimately suggest and promote the notion that there were positive means by which the workings of society could be changed for the better, such as the French Revolution.These were modern and often liberal tenets which were at least partly allied to emancipatory prospects.

The appearance of social evolutionary schemes in print during the 1750s represents part of a wider transformation in views of the world as known and seen from northern Europe. Once stated, it was readily acceptable among those who were in sympathy with other tenets of the time: the ideologies of progress and improvement, the possibility of source criticism of Classical authorities and even the Bible, and the sense that Europe was in the vanguard of history. This latter was possible because of the apparent differential economic and political achievements by nations within Europe, and also because of the

1. The sources of social evolution

wider comparisons made possible through increasing knowledge of especially the 'New World' and its inhabitants. There had been an earlier debate, primarily in France, about the so-called Ancients and Moderns, and whether contemporary achievements, initially mainly in the arts, could be said to have equalled or even surpassed those of Classical authors (Fontenelle 1708; Perrault 1964). It was an obvious extension of this debate to include material accomplishments – quantity as well as quality – and other peoples from the present as well as those of the past, and to attempt to order and explain them: the Enlightenment was a great period of systemisation and classification in all kinds of ways.

However, it still remains to be explained why the stages proposed focused initially on subsistence as the defining characteristic of past and present societies. If we had looked only at pre-1750 traditions, we might have predicted that climate or 'environment' would be the most likely to be elaborated. Montesquieu (1989), in his 1748 *Spirit of the Laws*, attempted to explain differences in 'national character' and hence governance – political economy – such as tendencies towards despotism or monarchism, largely through differences in climate. Both he and others were drawing directly on earlier and especially Greek sources. Why then should 'subsistence' have became the key?

Explaining difference

Social evolution is about the explanation of observed difference in perceived human achievement. At its simplest, this could be ascribed either to an unequal distribution of innate physical or mental endowments across groups, such as races, nations or genders, or to differences in external conditions. Prior to the eighteenth century, writers had often used a combination of the two, by admitting to national characteristics, but also invoking especially climate as provoking or maintaining particular responses. Thus hot climates were often seen as inducing or encouraging laziness, for example. However, in a spirit of rational inquiry many eighteenth-century commentators preferred to work from *a priori* assumptions about human nature. If humans were, broadly speaking, equally endowed, then the reasons for differential outcomes or progress had to be found in their responses to material conditions. What governed human practices? What were the underlying goals common to all people?

Clearly, argued early social evolutionists, the needs for food, shelter and reproduction were basic necessities. Given their interest in government and political economy, a fourth factor was often added: the need for defence, whether against wild animals or other people, and hence co-operation. For example, Goguet (1761: 84) wrote that 'At the commencement of societies, their first care would be to provide the necessaries of life.' After discussing hunting and fishing, he argued that 'the more industrious and discerning part of mankind' would observe the advantages to be obtained from confining and caring for the more tractable animals, and become herders. But he saved his greatest approbation for those who invented cultivation:

> It is to the discovery of agriculture we are indebted for that prodigious number of arts and sciences we now enjoy. As long as mankind had no other way of subsisting but by hunting, fishing, and feeding their flocks, arts made but very little progress. This kind of life obliged them to remove often from place to place, and did not require the knowledge of many arts. Those nations who do not practise agriculture, have still but a very slender acquaintance with the arts and sciences. The cultivation of the earth obliged those who applied themselves to it, to fix in a certain place, and to find out the various arts they stood in need of.
>
> Goguet 1761: 85

1. The sources of social evolution

Using very similar language, Adam Smith, according to lecture notes made *c.* 1763, reasoned that 'all the arts, the sciences, law and government, wisdom and even virtue itself tend all to this one thing, the providing [of] meat, drink, rayment, and lodging for men' (cited in Meek 1976: 126). In the same year Quesnay and Mirabeau, in *Rural Philosophy*, asserted that:

> Man in this world has only three primary needs: (1) that of his subsistence; (2) that of his preservation; and (3) that of the perpetuation of his species ... Of these three, the first is the only one which is imperative, indispensable, and individual ... Subsistence ... is therefore at the heart of the matter.
>
> Quesnay & Mirabeau 1962: 59

A little later William Robertson (1783, 2: 96-7) argued that 'in every inquiry concerning the operations of men when united together in society, the first object of attention should be their mode of subsistence. Accordingly as that varies, their laws and policy must be different.'

There was a close relationship between those who advocated agricultural improvement at home and those who commented upon the failures of savages to take best advantage of natural abundance and fertility. The argument was already made by the seventeenth century, but the connection is epitomised by Henry Kames, who wrote upon and practised improvement on estates for which he was responsible in Scotland, but was also the author of *Sketches of the History of Man.* Kames, like many others, argued that material necessity, intensified by population growth, drove social evolution. However, he also left room, as did Goguet, for ascribing inventions such as that of agriculture to individuals with more application and foresight than their fellows, and condemning others for their laziness. In a chapter tellingly entitled 'Progress of Men with respect to FOOD and POPULATION' he argued that 'Necessity, the mother of

29

invention, suggested agriculture. When corn growing spontaneously was rendered scarce by consumption, it was an obvious thought to propogate it by art' (1774, 1: 47). He continued:

> That the progress above traced [from gathering, to herding and then agriculture] must have proceeded from some vigorous impulse will be admitted, considering the prevailing influence of custom: once hunters, men will always be hunters, till they be forc'd out of that state by some overpowering cause. Hunger, the cause here assigned, is of all the most overpowering; and the same cause, overcoming indolence and idleness, has introduced manufactures, commerce, and variety of arts.
>
> Kames 1774, 1: 50

The examples above are all drawn from Scotland and France, though other examples could be drawn from elsewhere in northern Europe in the later eighteenth century. A slightly different trajectory can be seen in one of the great colonial powers in southern Europe, equally involved in observation and exploitation of the newly-discovered savages in the Americas. Britain and France, it should be noted, were interested in New World opportunities for colonial settlement as well as trade. In Spain there had been a greater focus on the direct extraction especially of gold, one of Colombus's primary interests, and a different understanding of what might constitute wealth. In the context of forced and slave labour in the Caribbean and elsewhere, one of the early debates had been the extent to which New World Indians were fully human to the extent of having souls which could be saved for God through conversion to Christianity. Thus Pagden (1986, 1993) notes that the starting point for many Spanish theologians of the sixteenth and seventeenth centuries, debating the moral and indeed human status of New World 'Indians', was the works of Aristotle and Aquinas's later commentary. Aristotle's anthropology was of particular interest because of his theory that some people could be distinguished as natural slaves. Given the ways in which the Spanish tended to exploit the Americas through forms of forced labour of the indigenous peoples, debate about the nature of the difference between Europeans and others was conditioned by the interests of missionaries and the Church, colonial settlers and their patrons, and the economic, legal and moral rights and duties of the monarchs. Questions about the relationship of native Americans to a Christian God could be answered in terms of a retained originary innocence, a loss or perversion of knowledge of the true God, or, as in the famous debate between Las Casas and Sepúlveda in the mid-sixteenth century, ascribed to differences in human natures including the susceptibility to conversion (Pagden 1986: 119-45). Explaining how these natural or cultural differences arose and persisted, however, increasingly involved history, though typically founded within a religious understanding such as Acosta's understanding of evolution within the Americas as preparation for the 'coming of the Spaniards' and the Word of God (Pagden 1986: 193).

The rise of racism

For a period of fifty years, social evolutionary schemes of the sort detailed above made their appearance in all sorts of 'histories' and were alluded to elsewhere (Meek 1976). By the early nineteenth century, however, there is a decline in the frequency of allusion and a shift in the nature of social evolution: different kinds of approaches are preferred. There are many political, cultural and economic, as well as intellectual, tendencies, which are associated with this shift in emphasis away from 'classic' social evolution and the rise of romantic and idealist philosophies of history. One factor is nationalism within Europe: competition in trade and empire between nations is also expressed in the way these are placed within histories which are used to bolster national identities. Another is the reaction to the French Revolution and its aftermath: the actual or perceived association of many French intellectuals, the *philosophes*, with the violence and atheism of the Revolution led to the restatement of conservative and religious beliefs and a distrust of radicalism. A third aspect relates to the changing conditions of colonialism and imperialism, and the changing relations with and perceptions of indigenous populations. As colonial settlements and systems expanded, initial conditions of encounter and enslavement were partly transformed into encapsulation and administration. In America the savages once beyond the frontier were increasingly becoming an internal 'Indian problem'.

Although one can identify racial stereotyping in the eighteenth century (Popkin 1973), it is during the nineteenth century that race becomes the preferred explanation and justification for differences and hence the basis for differential treatment. This meant that some of the basic assumptions of classic social evolution such as the unity of mankind in which some people *happened* to have progressed further could not be maintained: rather some were destined to achieve more, while others were doomed always to lag behind and were incapable of scaling the heights. It was debated whether the races had been separately created (polygenesis) with separate and unequal endowments. These mentalist and idealist understandings of what had enabled some groups, primarily nations and races, to progress further and more quickly than others were at odds with histories which laid emphasis on material conditions as the driving force of change and difference. Two writers from the German-speaking world neatly demonstrate the shift from the liberal tendencies of the Enlightenment, towards the potential excesses of romanticism and idealism: Johann Gottfried von Herder, and Georg Hegel.

32

1. The sources of social evolution

Von Herder was active in the second half of the eighteenth century. A theologian and philosopher, his *Reflections on the Philosophy of the History of Mankind* was published between 1784 and 1791 while he was at Weimar. Here, as elsewhere, Herder is absolutely explicit about his belief that all humans are of equal capacity and worth, and unlike his teacher, Kant, he rejects the idea of race, suggesting that 'all mankind are only one and the same species' and that 'upon the whole, all are at last but shades of the same great picture, extending through all ages, and over all parts of the Earth' (Herder 1968: 7). Herder appreciates – indeed respects and marvels at – what we would now call cultural difference, and the right of people to live as they would wish: this leads him also to condemn acts of colonialism in which Europeans entered the Americas, for example, 'as despots, arbitrarily practising violence and extortion' (Herder 1968: 12). Ways of life are conditioned by the environment, equally well fitted to local needs and deserving of equal praise. He refers directly to the categories of social evolution, but immediately expresses his doubts:

> It has been customary, to divide the nations of the Earth into hunters, fishermen, shepherds, and husbandmen; and not only to determine their rank in civilization from this division, but even to consider civilization itself as a necessary consequence of this or that way of life. This would be very excellent, if these modes of life were determined themselves in the first place: but they vary with almost every region, and for the most part run into each other in such a manner, that this mode of classification is very difficult to apply with accuracy.
>
> Herder 1968: 50

Later he adds: 'Let justice be done to other ways of life, which, from the constitution of our Earth, have been destined, equally with agriculture, to contribute to the education of mankind' (Herder 1968: 57).

Herder further extended this cultural relativism and argued that people (*Volk* – often translated as nation) should be allowed to live according to their customs. However, historically, the progressive expression of humanity was epitomised at various times in different peoples and places. But Herder was often inconsistent and uncertain whether such progress had occurred. For example, at one point he takes a Rousseauian perspective and argues that agriculture and particularly private ownership of land led to a 'frightful despotism' so that 'the oppressed, sunk in cowardice and slavery, were led from wretchedness and want into effeminate debauchery' (Herder 1968: 57). Elsewhere, however, he feels more optimistic, speaks explicitly of the moral and material progress within human history, and states that after the discovery of agriculture 'Man found, that he could live better, more decently, and humanely, on the pleasing gifts of Ceres' (Herder 1968: 110). In the *Reflections*, and elsewhere, Herder vacillates 'between several incompatible models of history's direction' (Forster 2001).

Forty years later, Hegel's *Philosophy of History* (1837) was published. Based on his lectures delivered at Berlin in the decade before his death in 1831, his outline of historical thought had been influenced by that of Herder. However, the east to west progress which Herder had (sometimes) seen as a contingent fact now became the organising principle of the *telos* of history, along with a heavily racialised explanation. 'The History of the World travels from East to West, for Europe is absolutely the end of History, Asia the beginning' (Hegel 1956: 103). He has no interest in the 'primitive', since for him this 'pre-history' has no bearing on World History as the expression of Spirit or Reason. For Hegel, true History was only manifested when certain advanced political conditions were present, at which point nations may be said to enter history, or become

1. The sources of social evolution

'World-historical' peoples. 'Freedom [i.e. the aim, essence and manifestation of World Spirit] is nothing but the recognition and adoption of such universal substantial objects as Right and Law, and the production of a reality that is accordant with them – the State' (Hegel 1956: 59). In conjunction with a Eurocentric attitude towards climate and alleged racial characteristics, vast areas of the known world, as well as many races and people, are deemed outside history. His particular mix of racism, quasi-mysticism and erudition set the pattern for many Romantic or Idealist philosophies of history to come.

> In the Frigid and in the Torrid zone the locality of World-historical peoples cannot be found ... The true theatre of History is therefore the temperate zone; or, rather, its northern half.
>
> Hegel 1956: 80

> America has always shown itself physically and psychically powerless, and still shows itself so ... The inferiority of these [native American] individuals in all respects, even in regard to size, is very manifest.
>
> Hegel 1956: 81

Even though Negroes are physically, and in potential for learning, superior to aboriginal inhabitants of America, argues Hegel, America's future part in History can only come via Europe. 'The original nation having vanished or nearly so, the effective population comes for the most part from Europe; and what takes place in America, is but an emanation from Europe.' (Hegel 1956: 82). Whatever the future may hold, it is the thus the Old World which is 'the scene of the World's History' (Hegel 1956: 87). However:

> Africa proper, as far as History goes back, has remained – for all purposes of connection with the rest of the World –

35

shut up; it is the Gold-land compressed within itself – the land of childhood, which lying beyond the day of self-conscious history, is enveloped in the dark mantle of Night.

Hegel 1956: 91

Hence Africa 'is no historical part of the world; it has no movement of development to exhibit' (Hegel 1956: 99). Such arguments are again compounded with racist perceptions:

The Negro, as already observed, exhibits the natural man in his completely wild and untamed state. We must lay aside all thought of reverence and morality – all that we call feeling – if we would rightly comprehend him; there is nothing harmonious with humanity to be found in this type of character.

Hegel 1956: 93

Asia is accorded respect as the source of some religious and political principles, but even the civilisations of China, India and Babylon are dismissed because of the people being 'shut up within themselves' meaning that 'a relation to the rest of History could only exist in their case, through their being sought out, and their character investigated by others' (Hegel 1956: 101), that is, when they are brought into History through European knowledge.

Thus although Hegel's philosophy of history is both progressive and calls on the name of Reason, it is very far from that of the eighteenth-century French and Scottish philosophers; his 'universal history' has shrunk to the story of the source and rise of Europe, and his conceptions of reason and of human nature exclude many more than they admit. As an empirically-based history, 'the true *result* of the World's History' (original emphasis: Hegel 1956: 21), the 'History of the World, the Idea of Spirit appears in its actual embodiment as a series of external forms, each one of which declares itself as an actually existing people'

Lo! as the fainting labourer stoops to reap,
The deadly drops his clay cold temples steep;
In pride of youth the Tyrant want prevails,
The sickle falls, and harrass'd nature fails.

Printed for Richard Phillips, New Bridge Street, Blackfriars.

Fig. 3. Exhausted labourers during reaping. Engraving by Anthony Cardon after De Loutherbourg, from S.J. Pratt (1807) *Sympathy, and other poems. Including landscapes in verse, and cottage pictures*, revised edition, London: Richard Phillips. The book is a mix of Virgilian pastoral and darker Georgic.

(Hegel 1956: 79; cf. Herder, above). However, Herder's respect for cultural traditions has been replaced by a racial hierarchy. Hegel thus has no need of a universal human nature from which he can, *a priori*, derive a conjectural universal history of mankind. Early stages of human existence, whether categorised through modes of subsistence or otherwise, have no place in Hegel's scheme and because of his peculiarly limiting vision of what comprises History, he has no interest in non- or pre-State societies.

Similarly, in France, the progress of Reason and mental attributes (as in Comte's stages of religion, metaphysics and then positivism [science]) were found to be of more interest than the materialist speculations of the Scottish School, and included innate racial characteristics as part of the explanation for geographical differentiation in achievements and histories (Stocking 1987: 28-30). Social evolution had not gone away, but it was differently understood. The trope of progress had become limited to particular nations or groupings. A materially-based universal history of mankind was less relevant for those whose world view rested on ideologies which were generally racist and which underpinned the maintenance and expansion of the nationalist, imperialist, colonialist and domestic *status quo* (Fig. 3), rather than promoting potentially emancipatory change.

2

Anthropology and archaeology

During the nineteenth century social evolution 'returned' in the guise of culture precisely as part of the newly-forming disciplines of anthropology and archaeology. While the social evolution expressed in the later eighteenth century became less salient in the first part of the nineteenth century, this is far from saying that the underlying idea of progress was rejected, but rather that other categories such as race and nation became more important. Andreski (1969: xxi) argues, like Meek, that the earlier social evolutionists had perceived such marked technical and economic change around them that they were driven to ask why and how it was occurring; but by the mid-nineteenth century writers 'began to take this onward march for granted'. Other factors include the fact that established religion was not congenial to the materialist underpinnings of classic social evolution (Stocking 1987: 45), but rather supported the notion of moral and spiritual superiority of certain Christian peoples, and this in turn was not necessarily antipathetic to the idea of the separate creation of the races (Stocking 1982). In a changing religious climate, and with the excesses of Reason and Liberty made clear by the aftermath of the French Revolution, national pride provided a new impetus for progressive Whiggish histories culminating in the author's present.

By the middle of the nineteenth century the sources and contexts for the interpretation of cultural difference had shifted. Firstly, it became more acceptable and empirically possible to adduce not only ethnographic, but also archaeological data to make arguments about the course and meaning of human history (Bowler 1989). Secondly, challenges to Biblical chronologies were increasingly accepted and the nature of historical as well as geological processes debated, as the length of prehistory was gradually extended (Chazan 1995; Trautmann 1992). Thirdly, new secular intellectual frameworks became available. Perhaps the most important of these was provided by Herbert Spencer, who used an organic metaphor for society, and a cosmic scientific framework for the directional rise of civilisation. Darwin's 'descent with modification', propounded in his 1859 *Origin of the Species*, was of much less importance, although it sometimes influenced the language people used. Certainly human history increasingly became thought of as a competitive race with winners and losers, so that one could reasonably apply Spencer's description of evolution as 'survival of the fittest' to societies or races.

Thus by the early twentieth century, in the first edition of his *Ancient Hunters and their Modern Representatives*, Sollas (1911: 382) infamously stated that the archaeological and anthropological facts 'teach in no equivocal terms that there is no right which is not founded on might ... the dispossession by a new-comer of a race already in occupation of the soil has marked an upward step in the intellectual progress of mankind'. In a recapitulation of seventeenth-century theologically-based justifications for colonial settlement, Sollas asserted: 'It is not priority of occupation, but the power to utilise which establishes a claim to the land.' For Sollas and many others, Biblical authority had been replaced by history understood as natural and secular rather than divinely ordained. So if a 'race' fell behind in its duty to exploit its strengths, 'whether in art or science, in breeding or organisation for self-defence, it incurs a penalty which Natural Selection, the stern but beneficient tyrant of the organic world, will assuredly exact, and that speedily, to the full.'

Views such as these underlay or provided justification for many colonial and imperial enterprises such as the scramble for Africa in the late nineteenth century. When couched in terms of race, the results in terms of practical policy could be at best paternalistic, with the 'lower races' treated for example as children needing guidance for an indefinite period (Jahoda 1999). Thus even J.S. Mill, in *On Liberty* from 1859, suggested that the doctrine of individual freedom need apply only to those 'in the maturity of their faculties' and should exclude not only children, but also 'those backward states of society in which the race itself may be considered as in its nonage [infancy]' (Mill 1974: 69). However, this devaluation of other races or cultures could also lead to indifference, gross exploitation or worse, even resulting in genocidal practices. It should be noted that this racial hierarchy also had a geographical expression: peoples were arrayed not only in time, through social evolution, but also within a Eurocentric space, with the most primitive people seen as at the 'uttermost ends of the earth' (Gamble 1992) such as Australia and Tasmania or Tierra del Fuego at the southern tip of South America.

Herbert Spencer (1820-1903) is often cited as one of the founding figures of the modern discipline of sociology, along with the French thinker Comte. He had an immense influence on people on both sides of the Atlantic, and is often blamed for enabling the nastier aspects of 'social Darwinism' (Degler 1991; Hofstadter 1992), the political creed that unbridled capitalist competition, whatever the social cost, was the best way to progress. Less controversially, he can be credited as the person who brought our modern understanding of the word 'evolution' into general use. Spencer ranged widely across science and history, and can perhaps best be described as a social philosopher. Actively publishing throughout the second half of the nineteenth century, he was seeking a 'universal expression' for 'structural modifications', and he found it in his own Law of Evolution, first expressed in 1857.

For Spencer, change was undoubtedly progressive, whether applied to physical or biological processes. He considered that 'existences of all orders' displayed both 'progressive integration' and simultaneously 'progressive differentiation' (quoted in Andreski 1971: 75). In Spencer's view, evolution 'could be discerned in all the realms of the universe, including inanimate nature' (Andreski 1969: x). Social evolution was just one expression of this cosmic law. In terms of human history, this meant that 'The change from the homogeneous to the heterogeneous is displayed equally in the progress of civilisation as a whole, and in the progress of every tribe or nation; and is still going on with increasing rapidity' (quoted in Andreski 1971: 78). Further, Spencer maintained that this progress was evident not only technologically, but also in the realm of culture – what he called the 'super-organic' – such as political organisation, language, painting, sculpture, poetry, music and dancing. This was a congenial message for many who accepted human history as showing a general trend of increasing social complexity and its positive valuation as progress.

Spencer's idea of evolution was organicist, and in his *Principles of Sociology* he generally offers an example from biology, often summarised from his *Principles of Biology*, before showing that human societies too can be thought of in the same terms. Evolution was basically dependent on the size of population (or organism) which thus necessitated differentiation of functions and hence complexity (Spencer 1969: 31-5). In human societies this is expressed through social organisation. The smallest and most nomadic groups are 'headless clusters' (1969: 32). But the first social differentiation occurs when aggregates reach about a hundred people, which necessitates a simple or compound ruling agency – typically a chief, but also seen in the sexual division of labour, for example. Here, as elsewhere, Spencer sees the need for defence as one of the prime factors: in many ways this echoes some of the earlier evolutionists who had argued *a priori* that the nature of evolution could be deduced from three or four basic necessities.

Spencer's stages are derived from a genealogy of types of social organisation, which he described as simple, compound, doubly compound and trebly compound – the latter being the 'great civilizations' (1969: 110-16). He is basically concerned with types of political organisation and the presence and nature of 'headship'; and although he distributes societies of various subsistence types throughout his categories, the simplest stages tend to include nomadic and foraging societies, and the more complex societies sedentary, trading and agricultural groups. This was basically a function of available food enabling larger populations: 'Where a fruitful soil affords much food, and where a more settled life, leading to agriculture, again in-creases the supply of food, we meet with larger social aggregates' (Spencer 1969: 24). Indeed, he explicitly says:

... we find reason for inferring that the changes from hunting life to the pastoral, and from the pastoral to the agricultural, favour increase of population, the develop-ment of political organization, of industrial organization, and the arts; though these causes do not of themselves produce these results.

Spencer 1969: 112

Spencer, however, adds a second cross-cutting categorisation of societies which he calls the 'militant' and the 'industrial' (Spencer 1969: 116-35). He argues that societies of the first type are generally highly centralised and social co-operation is com-pulsory; while industrial (i.e. trading) societies are typically decentralised with voluntary co-operation, which he relates, as befits a *laissez faire* liberal, to a free market and which he clearly prefers (Spencer 1969: 129).

Finally, however, there is a third factor which, tellingly, Spencer feels he has to include: race (1969: 130-5). Although historically produced, the 'deeply-organized character of the particular race' is 'very difficult to change' and greatly influences the type of society which will ensue. Another related and most potent determining factor is 'the mixture of races' present in any particular society. Circumstances 'where the two races, contrasted in their natures, do not mix' typically lead to compulsion and a militant type of society which is unstable: and, further, 'the half-caste, inheriting from one line of ancestry proclivities adapted to one set of institutions, and from the other line of ancestry proclivities adapted to another set of institutions, is not fitted for either ... and therefore cannot ... evolve any social type' (Spencer 1969: 132). However, small racial differences within a society 'seem advantageous'.

Spencer seems to encapsulate many of what we would now consider to be the virtues and vices of the nineteenth century. His range of sources in history, ethnography and elsewhere is prodigious. He fully admits the variety of factors which may affect social evolution: whatever the general tendencies of evolution, there are in any particular example complexities produced by the environment, tradition (which can thus lead to maladaptive traits in changed circumstances), and the political context such as surrounding societies (Spencer 1969: 130). His approach is thus comparative, and treats of cultural survivals and the effects of historical contingency. But ultimately the materialist underpinnings of subsistence and population size, leading to organisational complexity, are strongly inflected by race.

One important point to note about the later nineteenth-century theorists of social evolution is the lack of explicit allegiance to eighteenth-century predecessors, although this

2. Anthropology and archaeology

was more marked in Europe than America. For Tylor, for example:

> Criticizing an 18th century ethnologist is like criticizing an 18th century geologist. The older writer may have been far abler than his modern critic, but he had not the same materials. Especially he wanted the guidance of Prehistoric Archaeology, a department of research only established on a scientific footing within the last few years.
>
> Tylor 1871, 1: 48

Although these comparative ethnologists were undoubtedly aware of their forerunners, they tended to refer to them for empirical facts rather than adopting their schemes wholesale. In part we can see this as a turn away from purely material concerns. Late nineteenth-century writers were interested in the development of the social and moral aspects of history. Of necessity they turned to ethnographies and descriptions of classical societies, rather than either conjectural histories or archaeology, which had little to offer in this regard.

All accepted that there had been progressive change (Bowler 1989): how best then to reconstruct and eventually explain the historical sequence? In practice there was a combination of approaches and explanatory frameworks: the comparative method, the idea of cultural survivals, and diffusion were the most prominent (for a succinct summary of the underlying assumptions see Carneiro 2003: 9-25). The comparative method, in effect a typology arranged in time, was widely used, and was an explicit and much broader-ranging application of eighteenth-century and earlier practices, in which Native Americans in particular had often been used as examples of savages whose contemporary ways could illuminate the history of the more advanced peoples. 'In a sense, what social evolutionism did was to take the large masses of ethnographic data ...

and to classify them for another evidential purpose' (Stocking 1987: 108). Ethnographically-described peoples were ordered chronologically, that is, taken as more or less representative of 'earlier' or 'lower' stages of culture, either directly through what they lacked when compared with others – agriculture, or metal – or by taking as the norm western social institutions such as monogamy or monotheism and assuming that this necessarily represented the endpoint of a progressive teleology. On a smaller scale of analysis the doctrine of survivals suggested that existing and especially bizarre or apparently irrational practices 'carried on by force of habit into a new state of society' were 'proofs and examples of an older condition of culture' (Tylor 1871, 1: 15), a method followed particularly assiduously by Tylor and by Frazer in *The Golden Bough*. However, not all practices need be seen as having developed endogenously: diffusion was also admitted as a mechanism for change, though its popularity would reach its apogee early in the following century.

Despite the ever-increasing availability of empirical data from archaeology, geology and ethnography, the topics of interest of ethnologists such as religion, totemism, animism, mythology, family, property, kinship, law and the institutions of government had no obvious or direct archaeological correlates, though theoretically these were equally plausible categories through which to organise the 'simple to complex' classification at the heart of these Eurocentric histories and comparative ethnographies (Mandelbaum 1971: 96-7; Rowlands 1989). The vast array of characteristics which comparative anthropologists wished to use for societal classification went far beyond the subsistence regimes used in eighteenth-century schemes. Tylor (1865: 2-3) was most interested in questions 'such as the relation of the bodily characters of the various races, the question of their origin and descent, the development of morals, religion, law, and many others'. Six years later, discussing 'The development of culture', he acknowledged that while 'The principal criteria of classification are the absence or presence, high or low development, of the industrial arts, especially metal-working, manufacture of implements and vessels, agriculture, architecture, &c.,' all of which were potentially attainable from archaeology, he was keen to include 'the extent of scientific knowledge, the definiteness of moral principles, the condition of religious belief and ceremony, the degree of social and political organization, and so forth.' He went on to argue that practically and empirically it was difficult 'to reckon on an ideal scale the advance or decline from stage to stage of culture' Tylor (1871, 1: 25). For Tylor and others at this time the aim of comparative anthropology was the 'total study of mankind's progressive cultivation of mind, morality, refinement in tastes, and advances in technical skills ... Above all, the new science of man would focus on a history of the human mind' (Voget 1967: 133).

Even for McLennan, taught in Edinburgh, the Scots' conjectural histories were not his first port of intellectual call. McLennan identified three general themes for comparative anthropology: what we might now call socio-political organisation, technological and economic conditions ('the arts and sciences'), and religion and language (1869: 526), although he did argue that technical and economic progress was more accessible to study. McLennan, trained as a lawyer – many old-style stadial schemes occurred as prefaces to examinations of property law – and associated with the Scottish School, offers the most eighteenth-century sounding historical framework, though after brief reference (1869: 533-4) subsistence plays no further part in his interests or speculations.

One consequence was that the equation of hunters, pastoralists and farmers with the terms savages, barbarians and civilised peoples became temporarily decoupled. Lubbock, in his *Origin of Civilisation*, preferred throughout to use the phrase introduced in the first sentence: the 'lower races of men' (1870: 1). Tylor used savage, wild, rude and barbaric almost inter-changeably, and 'did not systematically distribute particular societies into these stages' (Leopold 1980: 38). McLennan (1869: 526) offered a political definition of civilisation, and 'savagery' was largely defined by default. Civilisation, he argued, referred to the fact of living in a *civitas* or state, and that 'strictly, we should not be justified in at all speaking of the stage of civiliza-tion of any people ignorant of the relations implied in citizenship'. However, in 1881, and perhaps influenced by Mor-gan's *Ancient Society*, Tylor formally defined savagery; barbarism, characterised by the presence of agriculture; and civilisation, which was signalled by the presence of literacy.

Archaeology and classification

By contrast, the newly-forming discipline of archaeology was initially concerned with categorising and arranging material culture in generally technological sequences. In Europe this first took the form of the familiar Stone, Bronze and Iron Ages. Although there were classical European and Chinese prece-dents for this sequence, the more immediate predecessors were to be found in early nineteenth-century Scandinavia and Ger-many. The first practical examples are those by the Dane Thomsen in his classification of artefacts, and in a regional survey by the Swede Nilsson in 1838-43 (Daniel 1964: 66; Klindt-Jensen 1975: 50-7, 65). In 1825 Thomsen wrote:

> I find it essential, in placing archaeological specimens accurately in context, to keep a chronological sequence in mind, and I believe that the validity of the old notion of first stone, then copper, and finally iron is constantly gaining new support in Scandinavia.
>
> cited in Klindt-Jensen 1975: 52

2. Anthropology and archaeology

The 'old notion' refers to Lucretius, rather than the conjectural historians of the previous century. However, Nilsson did follow the earlier pattern of mainly subsistence-based stages. Part of his work was translated into English by Lubbock and published in 1868 (Daniel 1964: 66; Rodden 1981; Rudebeck 2000: 94-9). Thomsen had in effect performed a simple seriation on existing collections and new finds: it had an empirical basis. This was expanded by those such as Lubbock in his *Pre-historic Times* when he divided the Stone Age into the Palaeolithic and Neolithic, using the presence of ground and polished stone tools as the type fossil of the latter. Given these separate sources, methods and interests among ethnologists and archaeologists, neither group felt the need to ensure a point-by-point correspondence with eighteenth-century stages. Burrow (1966: 117) notes that:

> palaeontology had shown a relationship between structural complexity and geological antiquity. Archaeology and [social] evolutionary theory might have become similarly associated, so that the chronological classifications of the one were the structural classifications of the other ... but there was no real correspondence between archaeological and anthropological classifications.

Lubbock and others (e.g. Tylor 1865) clearly intentionally rejected subsistence-based schemes for that of Thomsen. It was not immediately clear to archaeologists or comparative anthropologists what the relationships might be between material culture, technology and subsistence or other characteristics of 'savage' or 'barbarous' societies. For Lubbock the Neolithic always remained defined as 'the later or polished Stone Age; a period ... in which, however, we find no trace of the knowledge of any metal, excepting gold' (Lubbock 1870: 399). Thus although we can trace similarity of a sort between eighteenth-

49

and nineteenth century ideas, the intellectual genealogy is at best of an indirect nature. As Stocking (1987: 172) notes, it was 'by varying routes, [that] Lubbock, Tylor, and McLennan had each arrived in the early 1860s at the conjunction from which sociocultural evolutionism emerged'. The inability of archaeology to address the social and mental aspects of past societies promoted concentration initially on technological aspects of the archaeological record, and only subsequently on subsistence characteristics, when the hunter-gatherer/farmer divide was reintroduced by means of a redefined Neolithic. Barbarism construed simply as 'pastoralist societies' was clearly an archaeologically unsatisfactory category: it was variably used and sometimes overlapped with savage foragers, but not with literate urban-dwelling citizens.

It was not until the second quarter of the twentieth century that the archaeological Palaeolithic and Neolithic were explicitly equated to different modes of subsistence (Pluciennik 1998), although by the later nineteenth century it was increasingly referred to as an important distinction of importance, as in Tylor (1881). For example Dawkins (1894: 248) contrasted the nomadic hunters of the Palaeolithic, with 'Neolithic man' described as a sedentary farmer, potter, spinner and weaver, and miner who built tombs – the material elements of the Neolithic package. 'There is obviously a great gulf fixed between the rude hunter civilisation of the one, and the agricultural and pastoral civilisation of the other ...', he wrote. By 1916 Grafton Elliot Smith argued that 'the event which wrought the greatest and most far-reaching influence in the development of civilization was the acquisition of the art of agriculture' (Smith 1916: 498), which enabled large and settled communities. Agriculture alone 'transformed man's methods of existence and laid the foundation upon which the fabric of his material prosperity was built up. But it was even more fruitful in the realm of ideas.' This idea of a general association of farming with many other factors became established wisdom within and beyond archaeological circles. Thus Peake (1927: 21-2):

> It will, I think, be safer to divide mankind into producers and exploiters. The first group includes those who produce food and other commodities ... The second consists of those who gain their livelihood by exploiting the resources of nature, whether by hunting beasts and birds, large or small, or by collecting shell-fish, nuts, berries, or edible roots. The former group have, at least, started on the road to civilization, while the others are clearly uncivilized, even if we hesitate to call them barbarous or savage.

A little later Childe, who similarly distinguished the Neolithic by food production, extended this 'functional-economic classification' of stages to the other conventional archaeological periods – the Bronze Age with regular trade and specialised craftsmen, the Iron Age with 'cheap' tools enabling clearance, settlement and population expansion (Childe 1935: 7-9). Childe continued to use the terms savage and barbarian, referring to foragers and farmers respectively and separated by the 'Neolithic Revolution'.

Thus despite the apparent availability of a ready-made subsistence-based framework in the conjectural histories of the eighteenth century, the revival of social evolution in the 1860s in Europe was a complex reinvention. In keeping with the growth of systematic knowledge, nineteenth-century comparative methodologies were made far more explicit and authors were able to draw on newly-available archaeological evidence. Although their schemes fitted into notions of progress and hence also concerned the present and future of the human race (especially through social Darwinism), compared with their predecessors they were much more interested in the past and

difference for its own sake. This was part of the construction of
the new 'sciences of man', including the disciplines of anthropology and archaeology, and nationalist (pre)histories, as in
Scandinavia with the related early establishment of national
museums. However, in different political circumstances in
north America, the link between evolution, subsistence, morality and state policy was stronger, more narrowly defined and
more persistent.

Improving the natives: American materialism

In America there was a different trajectory. The existence of
Native and African-Americans within the polity was viewed
from a White Euro-American elite perspective, corresponding
to European attitudes towards colonial subjects. In the USA
this perspective was expressed in policies towards First Nation
peoples, an obvious focus for theories about origins, histories,
language and intellectual and psychological capacities in the
Americas. Such concerns and attitudes resulted in policies such
as the maintenance of slavery and later segregation, the removal of Native Americans to reservations and of their children
to separate schools, and the establishment of the Bureau of
Indian Affairs (originally part of the War Department) and the
Bureau of American Ethnology. The ways in which these policies were developed and applied depended on whether one
viewed 'Red Indians' and other races as of the same stock, or
separately created; whether they were capable of improvement;
and if so whether this would occur naturally or could be accel-
erated through intervention; and whether they would rapidly
disappear as an entity through inter-breeding with white
Americans – miscegenation.

In an America grappling with the 'Indian problem', a much
closer link was maintained between subsistence and 'proper'
ideas of property and morals, and expressed in policies to

educate and civilise Indians. Such practices had been taking place since the early nineteenth century (Gates 1971). Although there had been conflicting views about the true nature of the Indians and gross disparities between the views of some intellectuals and politicians, or between those on the east coast and the western frontier, for example, from the late eighteenth century the introduction of farming was seen as one solution to the Indian problem. In the 1790s Henry Knox, Secretary of War, argued that Indians 'were to be civilized by the adoption of private property, by the men farming in the American manner, by the women learning to spin and weave' together with education and Christianity. In 1808 Thomas Jefferson urged an Indian delegation: 'Let me entreat you therefore on the lands now given you to begin every man a farm, let him enclose it, cultivate it, build a warm house on it, and when he dies let it belong to his wife and children after him' (cited in Horsman 1968: 132-3).

Yet by the 1820s the realities of removal and the increasing desire for land had largely overcome any such scruples about essential equality, and the language of Euro-American superiority and racism was gaining the upper hand (Prucha 1969, 1971; Horsman 1975), although still in the 1840s and later influential voices were maintaining the idea of improvability. The eighteenth-century language of progress was maintained through colonial attitudes towards farming and land which would engender correct attitudes towards property. Practically, however, there was the *de facto* appropriation of land in the accelerating push westward.

This materialist bent and the belief in the importance and efficacy of subsistence practices was expressed in intellectual spheres by one of the key figures in America for ethnography and archaeology, Lewis Henry Morgan. Although most of *Ancient Society* (1877) is concerned with the development of social organisation and kinship – the growth of the ideas of government, family and finally property – Morgan's framework is his famous seven 'ethnical stages' (1877: 9-19):

Lower Savagery	Gathering
Middle Savagery	Fishing; use of fire
Upper Savagery	Bow and arrow
Lower Barbarism	Pottery
Middle Barbarism	Animal domestication (Old World)
	Maize cultivation, adobe & stone
	architecture (New World)
Upper Barbarism	Iron smelting
Civilization	Writing

The importance of subsistence or its material correlates is obvious, and Morgan made it clear that this was his ideal basis of classification:

> It is probable that the successive arts of subsistence which arose at long intervals will ultimately, from the great influence they must have exercised upon the condition of mankind, afford the most satisfactory bases for these divisions.
>
> Morgan 1877: 9

The whole of his second chapter is devoted to the 'Arts of Subsistence' in which he argues that:

> Mankind are the only beings who may be said to have gained an absolute control over the production of food ... It is accordingly probable that the great epochs of human progress have been identified, more or less directly, with the enlargement of the sources of subsistence.
>
> Morgan 1877: 19

Morgan's insistence on subsistence as the framework for

other aspects of society shows a strong relationship to materialist eighteenth-century schemata. Kehoe (1998: 175) notes that his closest friend was 'Josiah McIlvaine, a Presbyterian leader steeped in Scottish Common-sense Realism and the conjectural histories of Adam Smith, Ferguson, Kames, Monboddo, and their compatriots in Edinburgh and Glasgow'. Morgan (1877: 5) also excluded consideration of the development of religion – and speech – from his book, unlike his British counterparts, since 'Religion deals so largely with the imaginative and emotional nature, and consequently with such uncertain elements of knowledge that ... [t]his subject also falls without the plan of this work'. He also used race as a category, pointing for example to the superiority of Aryans, though at least in part because of their domestication of animals and consequent acquisition of dairy products. Such broadly materialist sympathies had obvious potential resonances for an empirically-based archaeology. But these were not the immediate concerns of American archaeologists attempting to come to grips with the extent, nature and chronology of the archaeological record in their 'New World'.

The ways in which American archaeology and anthropology developed were strongly influenced by the immediate presence of Others. For example, a discontinuity was seen between contemporary Indians and the archaeologically-known 'Mound-Builders' (Silverberg 1968) – were these latter the vanished equivalents to the civilisations of Meso-America? Later concerns with processes of acculturation and the culture and personality movement can all be seen as a direct reflection of engagement with issues such as the status and future of indigenous peoples and others. Turn-of-the-century mass immigration and the survival of Indian peoples and identities ensured that issues of acculturation – becoming American – remained an important topic. The intellectual, academic and bureaucratic structures of American anthropology were in large part formed by the consequences of practical and political policies towards Native Americans, and the four fields of American anthropology – ethnology, physical anthropology, linguistics and archaeology – were all initially concerned with elucidating the genesis and history of Native Americans.

By contrast, the relationship of European anthropologists to other peoples typically occurred far from home within colonial and imperial contexts and spheres of influence such as Francophone west Africa and the French Pacific, or the British in south Asia, Australia and east Africa. There was a form of distancing in which the geographical 'uttermost ends of the earth' were considered as equivalent to a chronological and evolutionary divide, and which tended to support forms of exoticism. However, prehistoric archaeology *within* Europe could be understood as part of a deepening of nationalist histories, of direct ancestors, no matter how remote in time and culture. Archaeology and anthropology began to develop their own concerns: their 'subjects' and indeed material remains were geographically and culturally remote from each other. The disciplinary relationship developed differently in north America, where common concerns and subject matter, physical continuities and the use of direct historical analogies meant that ethnographies and archaeologies, at least in a regional sense, could be taken as part of an historical continuum. Understanding where Native Americans stood in relation to a more general human history was part of understanding the role and future of an ever stronger, more confident and forward-looking United States.

In 1893 the American historian, Frederick Jackson Turner, presented an influential paper in which he considered the effect of the 'end of the frontier'. He argued that American character – what we might now call identity – had been largely forged through the pioneer spirit and physical expansion westwards; but that since the United States had reached the Pacific, this process was no longer operative. In Turner's view, the frontier was 'the meeting point between savagery and civilization' (1962: 3). Interestingly, from our perspective, he also explicitly offered a 'birds-eye' view of America in geographical and historical terms:

> The United States lies like a huge page in the history of society. Line by line as we read this continental page from West to East we find the record of social evolution. It begins with the Indian and the hunter; it goes on to tell of the disintegration of savagery by the entrance of the trader, the path-finder of civilization; we read the annals of the pastoral stage in ranch life; the exploitation of the soil ... in sparsely settled farm settlement; the intensive culture of the denser farm settlement; and finally the manufacturing organization with city and factory system.
>
> Turner 1962: 11

Such underlying assumptions were commonplace at this time, and were represented in other media, such as John Gast's widely reproduced painting of 1872, 'American Progress', in which Native Americans fled before The Spirit of Progress, shown leading the prairie schooners of settlers and the advance of railroads and telegraphs (reproduced in Berkhofer 1978, plate 8): a contemporary description glossed the picture as 'the grand drama of Progress in the civilization, settlement and history of our own happy land'. Sculptures showed white settlers arresting Indians engaged in savage acts, most famously in Horatio Greenough's Rescue Group from 1837, placed outside the Capitol, Washington DC, and Indians equally firmly placed in the past of a Euro-American future when more romantically portrayed as tragic and doomed, as in *The Last Mohican* of Fenimore Cooper.

At the same time responses to the 'Indian problem' ranged from indifference to suggested genocide, or 're-settlement' on

FOSSIL MEN

AND

THEIR MODERN REPRESENTATIVES.

AN ATTEMPT TO ILLUSTRATE
THE CHARACTERS AND CONDITION OF PRE-HISTORIC
MEN IN EUROPE, BY THOSE OF THE
AMERICAN RACES.

BY

J. W. DAWSON, C.M.G., LL.D., F.R.S., F.G.S.,

Principal of McGill College and University, Montreal ;
Author of
" The Story of the Earth and Man," " The
Origin of the World," etc.

THIRD EDITION.

𝕷𝖔𝖓𝖉𝖔𝖓:

HODDER AND STOUGHTON,

27, PATERNOSTER ROW.

MDCCCLXXXVIII.

Fig. 4. Frontispiece from Dawson's 1888 edition *of Fossil Men and their Modern Representatives:* the subtitle is a typical example of the ways in which contemporary peoples were equated to those of the prehistoric past.

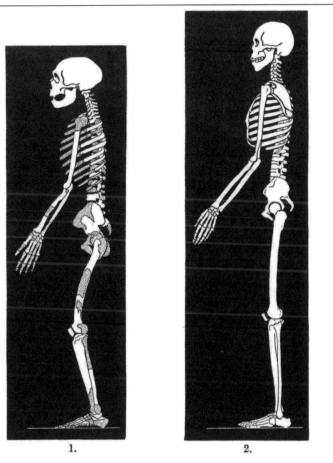

FIG. 117.—The skeleton of Neandertal man (1) restored according to Prof. Boule, for comparison with the skeleton of an Australian (2). (After Boule.)

Fig. 5. Illustration from the third edition of Sollas's *Ancient Hunters and their Modern Representatives* (1924). Throughout the book Sollas equates Tasmanian and other Australian aborigines to Neanderthal 'Mousterians' and Eskimos to Upper Palaeolithic peoples.

reservations, with land allotment and 'improvement'. What needed to be done with these backward and primitive peoples? The ubiquity of the notion of progress and social evolution meant that what went unquestioned was that Native Americans and others elsewhere were at a lower stage of development or simply the 'lower races', or 'our primitive contemporaries' (Murdock 1934) (Figs 4 and 5). Colonial and imperial attitudes towards indigenous peoples in administered territories were underpinned by hierarchies of race on the global scale, and class and gender on the national scale, so that only particular places and groups were seen as within progressive history. The dominance of western powers and capitalism, and anthropological and archaeological attitudes, mutually reinforced the ideas of value expressed through social evolution.

3

The fall from grace

Given the dominance of evolutionary frameworks in the second
half of the nineteenth century, it is perhaps surprising that the
first half of the twentieth century is often seen as anti-evolu-
tionary in tone, though this needs to be carefully qualified.
Nevertheless, we must ask: why was there an anti-evolutionist
reaction? What were the consequences? The answers are not
necessarily the same in Britain and the United States, nor for
the disciplines of anthropology and archaeology.

In pro-evolutionary histories of archaeological and anthropological thought in America the villain is seen as Franz Boas, the
most influential anthropologist in the United States during the
first half of the twentieth century. As Professor of Anthropology
at Columbia University from 1899, he and his students including Kroeber, Benedict and Mead are argued to have repressed
the legacy of Morgan's and others' work, to have introduced the
spectre of relativism into cultural anthropology in the States,
and to have generally denied the relevance of social evolutionism in favour of diffusion. Already by the end of the nineteenth
century there was the beginning of a strong reaction against
social evolution (Resek 1960: 155-8). The classic statement is
cited as Boas's (1896) paper 'The Limitations of the Comparative Method of Anthropology', in which he argued that
attempting to reconstruct a 'grand system of evolution of society' was of 'very doubtful value' and advised anthropologists to
abjure it.

But elsewhere it is clear that Boas's major problem with

61

evolution was rather the rigidity of the modes of classification. 'The grand system of the evolution of culture, that is valid for all of humanity, is losing much of its plausibility', he wrote in 1904. 'In place of a simple line of evolution there appear a multiplicity of converging and diverging lines which it is difficult to bring under one system' (Boas 1974a: 271). He often referred to the cultural bias informing the work of anthropologists and pleaded not for a supposedly unbridled relativism in its postmodern sense, but rather for critical awareness and a willingness to put aside subjective prejudices in favour of a scientific objectivity. Three years later he was perfectly willing to talk about investigating 'the sequence of events that have led to the establishment of the multifarious forms of human life' (1974b: 267), or the 'gradual development of new forms of civilization' (1974b: 270). What he suggested was that anthropology should enable us 'to recognize the possibility of lines of progress which do not happen to be in accord with the dominant ideas of our times' (1974b: 281).

Boas was undoubtedly a major figure at a crucial time in the development of academic and professional anthropology in the States. Given his primacy and the fact that many of his students subsequently became leading figures in or founders of other new anthropology departments, perhaps his influence was as disproportionate as some have argued (e.g. Carneiro 2003: 78). But a glance back across the Atlantic where there are some similarities in trajectory – though more a shift in emphasis than an outright rejection of evolutionary frameworks – suggests that other and more general factors were at work too. Kuper (1996: 5) notes the 'overriding concern with the accumulation of data. The ultimate goal might still be … evolutionist generalization, but … there was a feeling that the facts which were increasingly becoming available made facile evolutionist and diffusionist schemes look rather silly.' As part of this, there was an emphasis on work in the field rather than the armchair

(Kuklick 1997), which anthropologically formed part of a shift to study in person and in depth rather than breadth, and the outcome of which was a localised single-author monograph or detailed commentary rather than a sprawling comparative review. A concern with 'salvage ethnography' – recovering the facts before they disappeared – was evident on both sides of the Atlantic.

Secondly, diffusion as a mechanism of change became more prominent in Britain too. For example, at the end of the First World War Rivers recanted from a 'crude evolutionary doctrine' in favour of a diffusionism stimulated in large part by recent Melanesian fieldwork (Stocking 1996: 204). In Britain, Spencer was dead and Tylor retired soon after the start of the new century, and archaeology was becoming institutionally and intellectually a separate discipline. Malinowski and Radcliffe-Brown both expressed a distaste for 'survivals' and certain forms of historical reconstruction which they characterised as 'conjecture'. Explanation in their eyes primarily, though not exclusively, resulted from synchronic analyses based on field-work. The inter-relationships between existing institutions and customs in a society in question were best represented as an integrated and coherent whole, but as Ingold (1986: 74-102) discusses, this was not in any way a simple rejection of either evolution or history. Similarly in the States there was a focus on details and an emphasis on holistic views of individual cultures in the plural. In practice this often meant the dis-assembling of such cultures into individual features: any one culture was a particular combination of such traits.

In short, with the new century there was a general move away from comparative anthropology (and archaeology, in the States) and an insistence on the particular. Perhaps in part this was a necessary refocusing with the maturing and expansion in both numbers of practitioners and amount of data produced within the ethnographic discipline (cf. Clarke 1973 for archaeology). Many have argued that this historical particularism in the States and anti-historicism in British social anthropology was an over-reaction in which the pendulum swung too far. However, the attitude of Boasian anthropologists in the States was largely a product of concerns about meaning and priorities, rather than a denial of the data or overall framework. It was the start of a period in which the content of the term 'social evolution' changed from meaning the broad description of the stages of human history – which few if any challenged – to details of sequences for particular traits and the mechanisms by which change occurred.

'Boasian' students often adopted a comparative approach, as a way of putting forward generally liberal political inferences for the United States – pleas for tolerance, and critiques of unrestricted individualist capitalist *mores* (Benedict 1935; Mead 1943 [1928], 1942 [1930]). They were not against comparison *per se*; but disputed what the methods, goal and meaning of any such comparison should and could be. Of course cross-cultural comparison is not necessarily the same as a comparative anthropology aimed at elucidating social evolution, but neither is social evolution the only question in town. What the Boas School emphasised was that each culture group had its own values, and that individual traits or behaviours could not be understood without reference to the whole. One of the corollaries was that, by focusing on the specific, they were singularly unattracted to what they saw as over-generalising and unsustainable laws or causal processes. Anthropologists of the time did not question the broad outlines of social evolutionary history as expressed by archaeologists. For example Kroeber, in a general textbook current in the 1920s and 1930s, argued in familiar fashion that farming had 'freed men from the buffetings of nature; made possible permanent habitation, the accumulation of food and wealth, and a heavier growth of population' (Kroeber 1923: 414). Rather it was sequences such as those proposed by Morgan for kinship which were attacked (e.g. Lowie 1920). Within any one society the complexities of ethnographic data were seen to be too historically specific and integrated easily to lend themselves to fruitful large-scale comparisons and generalised sequences. Stocking (1996: 232) also notes the 'dehistoricization, ethnographicization, and professionalization' of anthropology which can be seen to occur on both sides of the Atlantic. By the second term he means the turn towards increasingly localised monographs. The third term refers to the 'development of more rigorous standards' for what constituted 'professional competence' in both disciplines, and the increasing inability of any single person, whether armchair anthropologist or fieldworker, to command all the relevant data. All these factors encouraged the institutional and intellectual fragmentation of a once-integrated anthropology. Interestingly, this also involved significant shifts in views on the significance of race as it became somewhat decoupled from culture(s).

In Britain, the separation of archaeology from anthropology led to the close association of universal human history with the former. A further context for this is worth noting: Stocking (1996: 367) quotes the British diplomat Lugard in 1922 writing on the changing nature of British imperial rule, in which the 'civilised nations' were the 'protectors and trustees of backward races' carrying 'the torch of culture and progress' and with a general duty of economic development, but also charged with looking after the 'material rights of the natives' and their 'moral and educational progress'. Practical imperatives, with Britain controlling a vast expanse of the globe, meant that a more hands-off approach to 'natives' had to be adopted, with paternalism or even limited self-governance under ultimate British control – British mandates or indirect rule. In this sense, anthropology has been seen as in an unsavoury relationship with colonialism and imperialism, with ethnographic knowledge potentially a tool for surveillance and management. Whatever the position of individual ethnographers, such attitudes were at least conducive to views which, even while fully accepting the framework of a progressive social evolution, judged the *utility* of social anthropology primarily as a survey of the here and now. This synchronic focus, whatever the causes and context, was expressed in the structural functionalism of Malinowski and Radcliffe-Brown.

In the United States the 'Indian problem' still provided a unifying pole for a four-fields anthropology, although here too funding for social anthropology directed at management issues, such as acculturation studies, may have encouraged the preference for synchronic analyses: how far had any particular tribe become acculturated? Which were coherent social entities capable of self-governance? Nevertheless divergences in, and increased amounts of, data and methods meant that practitioners within the four fields became more disparate in their interests. If archaeologists shared the tendency to investigate acculturation through the diffusion of culture traits, it became increasingly translated into descriptive regional typologies such as the famous Midwestern Taxonomic System. Particularism in archaeology often meant the avoidance of the 'big questions' and a retreat into culture history of a particularly sterile kind against which archaeologists such as White and Binford would later rail. 'Archaeology enjoyed little esteem and soon became the intellectual "poor boy" in the field of anthropology' (Willey & Sabloff 1974: 86), an inferiority complex which would be challenged precisely as part of the revival of social evolution. One of the claims of archaeology would then be that it could address issues of general social process because of its uniquely long-term and comparative perspective.

3. The fall from grace

The revival of social evolution

In 1939, at the annual meeting of the American Anthropological Association in Chicago, two papers were offered in defence of social evolution. In one, not published until much later, Alexander Lesser (1985: 78) admitted that social evolution as promoted by Morgan, Tylor and Spencer was currently 'as dead as a doornail in social anthropology', but went on to defend the principle and practice of formulating evolutionary sequences. The second paper was given by Leslie White, who had previously written in defence of Morgan. It was delivered before an audience including Boas, and was reportedly an impassioned attack on his principles (Carneiro 2003: 99-102). But it was largely post-war – Boas had died in 1942 – that the broad dominance of Boasian tenets in America began to decline, followed by the revival of neo-evolutionism and variously explicit forms of materialism, functionalism and empiricism (Trigger 1989: 275-328). The main lines of this evolutionary revival are well known: this 'neo-evolutionism' was originally expressed most influentially by Leslie White and Julian Steward.

White published throughout the 1940s and 1950s in favour of a revived evolution referring back to Morgan, Tylor and Spencer, but also with important differences. White suggested that there are three processes of interest to anthropologists: what he called the historical, the evolutionary, and the formal-functional (White 1945: 228; see also White 1938). According to White, history is concerned 'only with a chronological sequence of events, each unique in time and space' (White 1945: 229). By contrast the goal of formal-functional analysis was to arrive at generalisations across classes of events without regard to time or space (the example he gives is of insurrections). His evolutionist approach is also concerned with chronology, but only insofar as it allows reference 'to a sequence of events as a general process of transformation' (White 1945: 238). Although

White was at pains to stress that all three modes of analysis could be considered equally important, depending on the questions being asked, it is clear where his sympathies lay:

> ... the interpretation supplied by the evolutionist is more basic, more fundamental, than the interpretation of the historian or the functionalist. It is more basic because the evolutionist grasps and interprets events in their wholeness and entirety ... whereas the historian and the functionalist each deals with one aspect only – the temporal or the formal; they are thus partial and one-sided.
>
> White 1945: 244

White's divisions between levels of abstraction, and the singular and general, were in part themselves reactions to the nineteenth-century philosophical distinctions made between methods in philosophy, history and sciences. Clearly White (1938) wished to reclaim anthropology and archaeology for science in reaction against the prevailing culture historical and descriptive norms. He proposed that there should be a new name for a new scientific discipline – culturology (1949c: 409). He also suggested repeatedly that the 'evolution of culture' as a universal singular was somehow a thing apart from the evolution of cultures, which he called the culture history of peoples. He also proposed (1949a: 368-9) a Law of Cultural Evolution expressed as a formula: Energy x Technology = Degree of Cultural Development, summarising White's belief in what constituted progress: namely, that 'culture evolves as the amount of energy harnessed per capita per year is increased' or efficiency in so doing improves (see White 1959: 18-57 for a reworking of these formulas and ideas). White often used standard 'Old World' archaeological periods to exemplify cultural evolutionary stages as part and parcel of his technological determinism. He was influential through his persistent advocacy of evolutionism as a teacher and in print, and perhaps more generally in his claims that archaeology and anthropology could address big questions *scientifically* and take their rightful place: 'science cannot and will not stop in its forward march, in its movement of expansion, until it has fulfilled its potentialities to the utmost, and this means until it has embraced and subdued the whole realm of human experience' (White 1949b: 112).

Less obviously radical was Julian Steward. Having initially worked on foraging societies of the Great Basin, he later sought ways of categorising much wider ranges of society (Steward 1949). He suggested that a good method of cross-cultural analysis was, through what he called cultural ecology, to concentrate on the 'core areas' of cultures. Unlike White's technologically-based 'degree of culture', he offered a potentially more nuanced approach sensitive to cultural variation and limited parallels. Core areas comprised:

> the constellation of features which are most closely related to subsistence activities and economic arrangements. The core includes such social, political, and religious patterns as are empirically determined to be closely connected with these arrangements ... cultural ecology pays primary attention to those features which empirical analysis shows to be most closely involved in the utilization of environment in culturally prescribed ways.
>
> Steward 1955a: 37

This was in some ways a restatement of the materialist concerns of eighteenth-century writers, who had argued that the need to survive meant that subsistence should be the primary focus of attention. Steward is often praised for his multi-linear evolutionism – the fact that he was careful to lay down guidelines, rather than laws; and for his awareness of the potential complexity of societal responses and sources of change, and his pointing to parallel and convergent evolution as possibilities.

69

He rejected the 'universal evolution' of the nineteenth century and of White by suggesting that whatever their validity, the 'postulated cultural sequences are so general that they are neither very arguable nor very useful' (1955b: 17). He also attacked White's search for universal explanatory laws which would encompass 'all modes of behaviour' (1955c: 8). In its place he suggested a 'multi-linear evolution' which would investigate rather more limited patterns. Carneiro (2003: 110-15), a staunch supporter of White, has expressed disappointment that this later 'cautious, timid Steward' was in retreat from his initial 'bold, intrepid' position of the late 1940s, though admitting that Steward's later version 'being blander, was therefore more acceptable' to a generally sceptical audience (Carneiro 2003: 114-5). There were also other good reasons why Steward's evolutionism was welcomed: his emphasis on environment and subsistence as a way of investigating larger questions was attractive to empirically-minded archaeologists seeking a way out of a maze of descriptive typologies.

Although White and Steward are rightly seen as important influences, directly or indirectly, on both sides of the Atlantic, the traffic was not all one way. The work of Childe (1936, 1964 [1942], 1951), who presented broadly Marxist outlines of pre-history, was often referred to. In his last major contribution, *Social Evolution*, Childe commented explicitly on his search to make 'archaeological stages coincide with what sociologists and comparative ethnographers recognized as main stages in cultural evolution' (1951: 22). In 1942 he had argued that 'a single directional trend is most obvious in the economic sphere' where there were 'revolutionary innovations, each followed by ... increases in population' (1964: 29). He went on to use Morgan's terminology to equate savagery with a 'gathering economy', barbarism with food production, and civilisation with the development of cities, and to discuss the importance of Bronze and Iron technologies. Ten years later he retained the basic framework, but was less certain about the relationship of consequent social categories to the archaeological record, and placed greater emphasis on diffusion (1951: 161-79).

Nevertheless it is clear that, for Childe, the transformations promoting qualitatively different evolutionary stages – whatever the sources of the innovations – were important for their productive and demographic implications. The Neolithic Revolution 'permitted a substantial expansion of population. It made possible and even necessary the production of a social surplus. It provided at least the germs of capital' (1951: 22). The Urban Revolution, the development of cities, represented a 'revolutionary change in the scale of a community's size, economy, and social organization', enabling the 'accumulation of a social surplus' (1951: 24). Earlier he had noted the productive and population increase similarly associated with the Iron Age, with feudalism, and with the 'bourgeois capitalist' economy and industrial revolution (1964: 31-2). In *Social Evolution* he concentrated on the earlier parts of the archaeological sequence, but emphasised divergence and variation as well as convergence: 'the observed developments in rural economy do not run parallel; they cannot therefore be used to define stages common to all the sequences examined' (1951: 162). He drew back from an over-prescriptive typology: 'on the whole archaeology does not hold out much prospect of correlating social institutions with stages of cultural development as defined in economic terms' (1951: 165).

For some, Childe's approach offered a useful framework upon which to erect other developmental trajectories. For example, in a series of lectures Redfield (1953) used Childe as the archaeological basis for the argument that 'civilisation' represented, overall, a growth in moral sensibilities. 'On the whole', he argued (1953: 163) 'the human race has come to develop a more decent and humane measure of goodness'. This was enabled by the mixture of thoughts and new experiences made possible by the urban revolution: 'Only civilization could bring about the circumstances of moral conflict in which these [reformist ecumenical] ideas could arise and the means for their transmission and reflective development' (Redfield 1953: 83).

Other important figures in the development of neo-evolutionism and its impact on archaeology were Service, Sahlins and Fried. In *Evolution and Culture* Sahlins (1960) distinguished between general evolution – the overall pattern characterised by, as in White, the progressive ability to utilise greater amounts of energy and be less constrained by the natural environment, with consequent increased social integration – and specific evolution, which dealt with the sequences and processes of local and regional change. In the same volume, Service argued for a Law of Evolutionary Potential: that Progress (with a capital 'P') was normally discontinuous in societies and in space. Innate conservatism, meaning investment in a particular practice – the equivalent of biological specialisation – meant that those less committed to a particular tradition were often in a better position to take advantage of any innovation which might diffuse their way (Service 1971: 34).

In 1962, in a book dedicated to Steward and White, Service had described the outlines of the evolution of social organisation. By that term he meant the social structure – 'the component groups of a society and ... the configuration of their arrangement', and the 'network of statuses ... named social positions which are assigned conventional attributes and roles that regulate or influence the conduct of interpersonal relations' (Service 1971: 11). In his most succinct statement he added that:

The evolution of culture as measured by changes in social structure consists of a movement in the direction of greater size and density of the social body, an increase in the number of groups, greater specialization in the function of groups, and new means of integrating the groups.

Service 1971: 100

The mechanisms promoting types of adaptation or change were primarily environmental resources and political competition. Service went on to distinguish four types or levels of social structure. The simplest and earliest was the patrilocal band, which comprised related nuclear family units and demonstrated no specialisation or organisation beyond that of kinship. It was basically confined to foragers. Tribes, his next type, may have developed in unusually rich areas during the Palaeolithic, but were generally a feature enabled by the 'neolithic revolution' and hence 'much more effective control over the natural environment' (Service 1971: 99), including improved and more consistent productivity.

Although still egalitarian and familistic, tribes were larger and required additional means of cohesion, offered by 'pan-tribal sodalities', which may or may not have been derived from kinship relations. Service argued that, given the necessary productive resources, warfare and inter-tribal competition were the factors which promoted and maintained unity. The third level, chiefdoms, proved a particularly stimulating innovation to archaeologists since they seemed to offer possibilities for material correlates (e.g. Renfrew 1973a, 1973b): they were to be qualitatively distinguished by economic, social and religious centres, marked economic specialisation and redistribution 'with a permanent central agency of coordination' (Service 1971: 134) which also played a social, political and religious role. Typically, they were encouraged by natural variation in productivity within a small region which thus promoted redistribution among sedentary peoples, although secondary chiefdoms could be stimulated through competition. They were hierarchical and inegalitarian, and included permanent offices including that of a chief. Finally states, which

73

Service spent little space discussing, were distinguished from chiefdoms by their ability to monopolise force, the presence of political and socio-economic classes, and 'bureaucratic governance' (Service 1971: 163-7).

The work of Fried (1967), often cited but less often operationalised by archaeologists, at least, shows both similarities and differences to that of Service. He explicitly criticised Service's and Sahlin's notion of tribes (Fried 1967: 164-74), placed greater emphasis on the distinction between pristine and secondary polities and less on kinship *per se*, but still maintained the broad correlations between environment and subsistence type and levels of society, again ultimately because of the potential for productivity and population growth. However Fried preferred to work with the concepts of ranking and stratification. 'A rank society has means of limiting the access of its members to status positions that they would otherwise hold on the basis of sex, age, or personal attributes' (1967: 52). Such positions may or may not be associated with economic status. In stratified societies, by contrast, 'the adult members of a society enjoy differential rights of access to basic resources'. These two types of society were preceded by egalitarian societies, equivalent to the band level of Steward and Service, which Fried characterised largely by what they lacked – restrictions on access to resources or land, on group membership, institutionalised leadership, law or military organisation (1967: 58-106).

Once again, the emergence of rank societies is ultimately dependent upon the availability of food, primarily enabled by the 'neolithic revolution' and consequent increase in population spread, size and density. Rank societies are characterised by a redistributive economy. Politically, the differences between rank societies and their predecessors 'are essentially based upon varying increments of prestige and upon the hierarchical ordering of status positions' (1967: 183). This in turn is due to the growing size and spread of societies and the need for a more wide-ranging integration and organisation. The key factors for Fried were therefore 'ecological demography and the emergence of redistribution'.

Fried has been most criticised for his concept of stratified societies, which he admitted are an unstable form 'almost impossible to find' in the ethnographic record, and which almost inevitably led to fully-fledged states or back to rank societies. Restriction of access is in effect about the institution of private property in basic resources, and Fried suggested that it may have developed in response to population pressure and consequent changes in land tenure, altered availability of basic resources due to changes in the natural, external political, or technological context; changes in residence patterns, or the development of managerial roles (Fried 1967: 196). With this latter point he was already alluding to what others (e.g. Wittfogel 1957) had discussed in relation to the origin of the state, and it is difficult to separate Fried's stratified and state societies. Functionally, the institutions of a state exist to maintain stratification. However, 'The state must maintain itself externally as well as internally, and it attempts this by both physical and ideological means, by supporting military forces and by establishing an identity among other similar units' (Fried 1967: 235).

Carneiro continues to be a staunch defender and scholar of Spencer's and White's approaches to evolution, though his own contributions have been seen as most important in relation to modes of cross-cultural analysis such as scale analysis, where the sequences in which particular traits appear are argued to be highly regular and cumulative (Carneiro 2003: 157-9). He has also offered important papers relating to the ways in which ecological and socio-political circumscription, that is, the loss of a mechanism of fissioning, may lead to population pressure and associated tensions demanding an organisational resolution (Carneiro 1970, 1987).

Harris's 'cultural materialism' was an explicit attempt to provide a fundamentally Marxist perspective for American anthropology, but at the same time to react against structural Marxist approaches deriving primarily from western Europe. As part of his 'back to basics' he posited 'bio-psychological constants' of human nature – essentially greed, laziness, and the desires for sex and for affection (Harris 1979: 63). He also introduced a mode of reproduction, meaning the configuration of demographic processes. Harris used a distinction between the etic, externally observed and recorded data, and emic, using values and categories internal to those being studied. Etically, the modes of production and reproduction constituted the Infrastructure; the domestic and political economies the Structure; and such behaviours as arts, rituals, sports and science the Superstructure (Harris 1979: 53). There was a parallel set of emic understandings, which he lumped together as the 'mental and emic superstructure' (Harris 1979: 54). While he was at pains to point out that structural and superstructural elements might play a role, he argued for a 'principle of infrastructural determinism' which initially assumes that 'infrastructural variables are the primary causal factors' (Harris 1979: 56). This was because biological and material constraints meant that infrastructure formed 'the principal interface between culture and nature, the boundary across which the ecological, chemical, and physical restraints to which human action is subject interact with the principal sociocultural practices' (1979: 57).

The outcome of Harris's framework is a social evolution in which ecological conditions and consequent cost-benefit calculations explain the shift from one social level to another, as well as their variation. Despite the sometimes different terminology and genuine innovation, the emphasis on ecology and demography appears familiar, with egalitarian forager bands, 'big-men' village societies, chiefdoms and states showing increasing hierarchy, centralisation and control. Elsewhere Harris (1978: 8) argued that human history comprised a series of cycles of 'reproductive pressure, intensification and environmental depletion' which could explain the direction and nature of social, political and cultural change and variation.

Johnson and Earle (1987, revised in 2000) provide another example of how, perhaps, in much social evolution, *plus ça change, plus c'est la même chose.* Dedicated to Marvin Harris and Marshall Sahlins, *The Evolution of Human Societies* is a substantial review of ethnographic and archaeological literature, and its theoretical perspective is an integrative one, attempting to unite, or use as complementary, perspectives from economic anthropology, ecology including optimal foraging theory, structuralism and materialism. However, like Harris and many of their predecessors, their discussions are rooted in population growth as the 'primary motor' which necessitates subsistence intensification, leading to both social stratification and economic and political integration (1987: 15-17; 2000: 29-32).

> The pressure of an increased population on resources evokes a set of economic and social responses that interact to create a higher level of economic effort capable of sustaining an increased population. The process repeats itself until eventually a growing population becomes possible only with the increasing involvement of leadership, with its concomitants of increasing dependence and political development.
>
> Johnson & Earle 1987: 15

Again they attempt to describe (2000: 32-37) the characteristics which typify each of their levels of 'socioeconomic integration', namely, the Family-Level Group, the Local Group (including Big Man societies), and the Regional Polity, which includes chiefdoms and states. But – given that such transformations may easily be read as an erosion of social and political autonomy – why, they ask, should families (households, kin groups) consent to such integration? They answer in cost-benefit terms. Although political symbols may help to 'create and maintain a sense of unity' beyond the family, there must also be 'real, material benefits' (1987: 323). 'The steady increase in population density that underlies cultural evolution creates problems that only the group can solve ... increasing population density causes the benefits of group membership for the family to rise correspondingly' (1987: 325; cf. 2000: 28).

The details of the arguments by White, Steward, Service and others following in their footsteps are easily available in their published works. What is of more interest here is why in the decades following the Second World War there was a gradually increasing acceptance that the process of social evolution was again not only a legitimate subject for study but also a potentially answerable question. However, one must note, as Trigger (1998: 124) points out, that neo-evolutionism 'never became the majority position in American anthropology', although for a time it 'dominated prehistoric archaeology'. It was perhaps partly as a reaction against racism after the genocides of the first half of the twentieth century that the post-war theorists of social evolution wanted to place it on an objective and scientific footing. In the United States those such as Fried, Service and Sahlins offered new stages and categories of social evolution related to socio-political and economic organisation, rather than either race or, at least superficially, subsistence. In the climate of the Cold War and the growing economic superiority of America, the reasons for the rise and fall of states and empires retained prominence in archaeological research, as did interest in the origins of agriculture in south-west Asia and Meso-America. Archaeological definition and identification of origins and stages, especially of farming societies and states, continued to be a major concern of many, and the end result was still often understood within an implicitly value-laden hierarchy of place and time.

However, from the 1960s onwards a combination of factors including post-colonialism, the revival of indigenous and other political activism, and shifts in the intellectual climate among western liberals led to various critiques or reworkings of social evolution. These include subaltern histories, Afro-centrism, the rejection of 'western' histories and values, and a turn away from cross-cultural comparative studies towards local and regional research. From the 1980s onwards the value of the longest-lasting categorical division derived from social evolution, that between foragers and farmers, has become increasingly questioned in both archaeology and ethnography. Yet for many this is not a rejection of social evolution, but rather a refocusing on other questions and scales of analysis. In more public and political spheres, works such as Francis Fukujama's *The End of History*, or the glossing of acts of global terrorism as an assault on 'civilisation', show that explicit social evolutionary thought still holds sway.

One argument for the change in emphasis would be to posit some general shift in *Weltanschauung* between the first and second halves of the twentieth century. The horrors of the First World War as experienced in Europe and the subsequent Depression promoted a sense of pessimism and perhaps encouraged a turn away from any easy reading of the past as progress. However, the aftermath of the Second World War rather resulted in a 'never again' response to the Holocaust and other events, which was expressed in various attempts at radical political and intellectual reform, including statements about and shifts in definitions of human nature, such as those from newly-established international organisations such as UNESCO (Malik 2000: 134-47). Trigger (1998: 124) points to post-war economic conditions in much of Europe and in America, with two decades of prosperity and growth once more encouraging 'a readiness to believe that there was an upward-moving pattern to human history and that technological progress was the key to human betterment'. Such optimism was to become tempered in the 1960s and after, but it is now clear that in many disciplines, and not just archaeology and anthropology, there was once more a widespread belief in and desire for the ability to manage, control, explain and even predict the course of human events, primarily through an avowedly scientific approach. Thus Service (1971: 31), like White following Tylor, wrote that 'One of the virtues of the evolutionary view is that, more than any other perspective, it makes the concerns of cultural anthropology directly relevant to modern life ... the study of the evolution of culture ... will enable us to forecast the future'. Smith (2003: 97-8) places the evolutionary arguments over definitions of the state and formation processes in the context of the Cold War. 'One can see the conflict between these accounts as ... a search for the historical legitimacy of competing conceptions of the State', and hence again, one might suggest, as much over interpretations of the present and goals for the future as investigation of the past.

The model for much of the humanities and social sciences was that of the so-called 'hard sciences', and especially physics, seen by many as the epitome of a quantified and mathematicised system of knowledge. This would reach its peak in the 1960s and 1970s, with not only New Archaeology, but also for example history and cliometrics, and the New Geography, all affected by the 'physics envy' described by Massey (1999). Archaeologists straddling science and humanities were perhaps particularly prone to see their intellectual salvation in the practice and rhetoric of the former. It offered a way to compete intellectually and institutionally with apparently more theoretically sophisticated ethnographic colleagues who were seen as dealing with 'softer' data (cf. Willey & Sabloff 1974). In the United States there had been an often-expressed antipathy to history by anthropologists. This can be seen partly as a continuation of Boasian particularism which in effect reduced history to genealogies. Ingold (1986: 74-102) offers an incisive discussion of the complex philosophical and terminological differences and misunderstandings underlying the conceptions of history, Spencerian and Darwinian evolution and science put forward by Boas, White, Kroeber and others. Ingold (1986: 90) suggests that 'we find in the writings of Boas, Radcliffe-Brown and White just one sense of history: it is a chronological sequence of empirical events'. Further, these and others can be broadly characterised as positivists. The 'tedious job' of the historian or archaeologist would be to collect specific facts, while it remained for the evolutionary scientist to present general and explanatory laws. If, then, anthropologists wished to aspire to the desirable status of scientist, it was argued, they would have to contribute to the latter goal. The effect of this general climate was later commented upon by Braidwood (1981: 24), who had himself worked on one of the great social evolutionary questions, the origins of agriculture: 'I think that in the US at least, the growth of the "new" archaeology, with all its scientism, will eventually be understood in part as a response to the growth of the NSF [National Science Foundation] as a source for substantial financial support for archaeology … It was important to behave and talk like a scientist.'

In general the immediate post-war consensus was one of a tempered optimism about technology: the benefits were apparent to many, though their source was increasingly depersonalised. Trigger (1998: 141) argues that evolutionary frameworks of the time presented largely reactive or adaptive perspectives on social change, and that:

By downgrading the role of both social relations and individuals as agents of change, neo-evolution was forging a view of progress that was more in accord with the corpo-

81

rate capitalism of the 1950s than was the parallel evolutionism created in the context of the more individualistic early industrial capitalism of the nineteenth century.

The literature on states and social complexity shows how, in north American archaeology, initial neo-evolutionary concerns with environmental parameters and adaptation such as cultural ecology shifted in the 1970s towards an interest in 'administration, as a theory of social evolution ... based on information processing and decision-making hierarchies was developed' (Chapman 2003: 69). There were, however, overlapping and sometimes contradictory currents regarding the role and status of societies defined in social evolutionary terms, which became increasingly visible throughout the 1960s and 1970s. Many in wider western society were increasingly concerned about the nature and effects of modern politics and practices, whether they were explicitly anti-capitalist or not. Political activism was manifested in various ways, from 'hippies' and Flower Power to the mass demonstrations of 1968; the prominence of Native American groupings and protests; a new wave of feminism; and the stirrings of Green politics. These concerns can be seen in a string of popular as well as academic books: Carson's (1962) *Silent Spring*, Ehrlich's (1968) *The Population Bomb*, Brown's (1972) *Bury My Heart at Wounded Knee*, Schumacher's (1973) *Small is Beautiful*, tellingly subtitled 'A study of economics as if people mattered'; and we could also add Marvin Harris's (1977) *Cannibals and Kings*. In relation to prehistoric hunter-gatherers, the geographer and palynologist Simmons has even claimed that:

At one time in the 1960s, for example, the notion that Mesolithic cultures might be responsible for the recession of forest was unacceptable to some members of the Quaternary Ecology community, and various methods, it was alleged, were deployed in order to prevent the evidence from being published in high-profile journals.

Simmons 1996: 230

Revisionism was in the air. In academic and disciplinary terms this was expressed by revisiting of basic categories and definitions. Chapman (2003: 69) suggests that in the 1980s and 1990s, partly due to the explicit incorporation of a variety of Marxist perspectives, social evolutionary debates included the roles of ideology, and more generally 'power and political strategies, conflict, control and exploitation'. Chapman is concerned with entities most often described as chiefdoms and states, or 'middle-range' societies. However, this broadening of the terms of debate and the causal factors and characteristics involved can also be seen in relation to the baseline for social evolution, hunter-gatherer bands. In the wider cultural sphere revisionism often took the form of a neo-romanticism. The ills of industrial society were contrasted with a generalised happier and more self-sufficient form of life in harmony, ecologically and spiritually, with nature, and of which Native peoples were often seen as exemplars.

Academically, at what is often seen as a landmark conference in hunter-gatherer studies Sahlins (1968) suggested that in terms of labour and material requirements foragers could be seen as the 'original affluent society', a point apparently reinforced by subsequent ethnoarchaeological work in southern Africa (e.g. Lee 1979). This inversion of expectations could clearly be used, for example, to query White's equation of social progress with the amounts of energy used, and in many ways fitted better with more general concerns about the consumer culture. By the 1980s this re-evaluation of hunter-gatherers was continued by distinctions between forager societies (e.g. Woodburn 1980) including division into simple and complex types (Price & Brown 1985), though these could as easily be interpreted as evolutionarily sequential rather than an expression of variation.

Others questioned the distortion which a social evolutionary framework can imply for the study of such societies. For example, in 1992 Dennell had criticised the use of stadial schemes in relation to the transition to farming in north-east Europe, when it led to some societies being described as in a 'state of transition' between foraging and farming for two millennia, rather than being studied in their own right as stable and persistent forms of life (Zvelebil et al. 1998: 3). Shennan (1993: 53) suggested that social evolution had promoted the 'deeply ingrained view that [non-state societies] are evolutionary stepping stones' and the 'associated tendency to look at them from an unsatisfactory teleological point of view as containing the seeds of future states'.

As those debating chiefdoms and states engaged with the complexities of regional sequences and ethnographically and historically known variation, two basic strategies emerged. Some preferred to sub-divide societal types in an attempt to reach greater precision; others to do away as far as possible with pre-determined categories in favour of broad descriptions such as 'middle-range societies', and to focus rather on distributions of traits, common strategies or identifying axes of variation. Chapman documents the steady inflation in types of chiefdom proposed; and by the late 1970s it was possible to list at least fifteen types of state (Cherry 1978: 413). Chapman (2003: 43) notes that typologies of this sort are far less common for 'bands' and 'tribes', arguing that this is perhaps due to 'recognition of the increasingly marked variation in social and political complexity, and its material expression, in chiefdoms and states'. However, other factors may be at work here: even if we accept that the range of archaeologically-visible material culture is generally smaller in the former two categories, there is an impressive number of factors which have been suggested

3. The fall from grace

for the transition to agriculture, often glossed in social evolutionary terms as the move from 'bands' to 'tribes'. Gebauer & Price (1992: 2) list thirty-eight. Even if we exclude those considered academically fringe, such as extra-terrestrial influence, one could posit an impressive number of permutations of traits which favoured one trajectory over another. This relationship between complexity and cultural variation is itself far from straightforward.

4

Other traditions

There are other ways of perceiving, explaining and narrating history. Because of our location and the perceived dominance of our intellectual tradition, it is easy to forget or ignore philosophies of history which do not depend on progressive social evolution. One would be the earlier western world view which emphasised degeneration from a Golden Age; another would be eastern philosophies which are characterised by a cyclical view of history. Where alternative conceptions do exist in our societies they are often from the minorities or the otherwise marginalised, such as the romanticised views of eco-friendly foragers promoted by environmental activists. However, each of these meta-narratives implies particular values for not only the past, but also the present and future. Attitudes such as nostalgia, fatalism, optimism, or the characterisation of existing or past peoples as primitive or as role models are ultimately based upon philosophies of history of which progressive social evolution is only one. All have intellectual, disciplinary and political implications in the present.

There are many different ways of producing histories, which may apparently invoke different concepts of time. However, the ethnographer Gell has persuasively argued that the experiential and phenomenological dimensions of time are common to humankind, and that cultural variation occurs rather in collective and societal 'representations of what characteristically goes on in the temporal world' (Gell 1992: 36). For example, discussing one particular group, the Kédang, who have been characterised as possessing a distinctly cyclical notion of time, he suggests that:

> The relevant distinction does not lie between different 'concepts of time', but different conceptions of the world and its workings. The Kédang do not believe that the world changes much or in very important ways, by contrast to ourselves, who are perhaps inclined to believe that the world changes constantly and in ways that matter a great deal.
>
> Gell 1992: 36

It is these characteristic ways of representing the way things are – the way the world 'works' – which enable us to speak of different types and philosophies of history. Following Gell, we do not have to insist upon contradictory or incommensurate concepts of time, but rather a range of representations of temporalities, processes and past, present and future events. Many of these representations can co-exist, depending on context and interest, within the same communities. Judgements about what comprises repetition, periodicity, sequence, duration, tempo and scale may be applied variably and selectively to different categories of historical entities, forming a complex matrix of possibilities.

The forms of history

Useful discussions of some of the forms which written histories characteristically take, primarily dealing with western historiography but with wider import, have also been offered by White (1981) and Mink (1981), among others. They suggest that distinctions can be drawn between types which they characterise as annal, chronicle and narrative. For White, annals are sequences of apparently unrelated events, such as the lists associated with some early medieval monastic writings, for example. Chronicles, by contrast, have a central theme or subject: for instance, a genealogy or sequence of kings. Finally, he points to the narrative form, the focus of his main interest. Through a particular form of emplotment, narrative treatment offers a moral judgement, and as a 'fully realized story ... endows events ... with a significance they do not possess as a mere sequence' (White 1987: 14).

Earlier White (1973) had suggested that in recent western historiography it is useful to recognise four major plot types or meta-narratives drawn from literary criticism: romance, satire, comedy and tragedy, which each tend to be associated with specific types of figurative language and forms of argument to produce particular worldviews or political ideologies; but even so he recognises that the associations are only tendencies. Historical narratives including the archaeological tend to be complex mixtures of elements, characters and arguments, though it can be argued that progressive social evolution with its common theme of humankind's heroic transcendence is most like White's Romance (Pluciennik 1999). What White's proposed narrative forms all tend to do is to produce a sense of closure, an end to the story. However, there are other ways of plotting history.

An instructive contrast can be made with other literary, historical and philosophical traditions. Some have noted that Chinese historical thought, whether from a Confucian, Taoist or Buddhist perspective, is nested within cyclical cosmological and historical frameworks (Bodde 1981). Unlike European and some other Asian systems which ultimately refer to an act of personal creation by a named god, these Chinese systems do not even have a fixed starting point from which to measure events (cf. Black 1989: 40-1). Nonetheless, this does not mean that such cyclicity precludes linearity in other aspects of Chinese histories at a variety of scales. For example, says Bodde (1981: 245), a widespread Confucian notion 'sees the days of the ancient sage-kings as a truly golden age, and all human history since that time as a process of steady degeneration'. Similarly for most Taoists the earliest times were also better, partly because of a lack of government, potential repression, despotism and labour: people were living in a 'state of nature'. Thus although history may ultimately be cyclical, the writers are living in the downswing portion. However, Needham emphasises the linearity of much Chinese thought about historical, rather than cosmological, time, in contrast to Indian traditions. The second century BCE *Huai Nan Tzu* has a chapter 'devoted to proving social change and progress since the most ancient times, with many references to material improvement' (Needham 1965: 23, n. 2). He notes that many Chinese thinkers displayed an interest in dynastic, linguistic and even archaeological histories, including Yuan K'ang's first-century CE proposal of a Stone-Bronze-Iron sequence (Needham 1965: 34-8).

While Needham explicitly contrasts Chinese and much later western European ideas about prehistory, Bodde argues that overall Chinese historical thought contains few references to linear progressivism as a philosophy of history. Citing Ho Hsiu from the second century CE, who proposed that history would take the form of three ages of Disorder, Approaching Peace, and Universal Peace, Bodde proposes that this is the first Chinese text which 'explicitly recognizes the possibility of positive human progress according to a fixed pattern of historical evolution'. However, in his view subsequent philosophers largely reject such interpretations, until the influence of European views about evolution and political theory. Overall, the impression given by scholars is that while certainly linear and even explicitly progressive concepts of history and of social evolution are clearly possible and present within the mass of Chinese historical thinking, they do not become dominant until the last century or so.

In southern Asia Hindu and Buddhist cosmologies place us as living towards the end of particular periods characterised by darkness and degeneration (Dumont 1965). Within vast cosmological cycles covering billions of years (Layton 1989: 6-7; Paddaya 1995: 113), each sub-cycle typically incorporates not progress but decline. 'Progress' is compressed into instantaneous, between-cycle, rebirth or re-creation, but on human or historical time-scales there is a 'continuous decadence upon all planes – biological, intellectual, ethical, social, and so on' (Eliade 1991: 113). While many have argued that this emphasis on destruction and regression inhibited ideas of *telos* or linearity in history, again the presence of these cosmological cycles did not preclude more pragmatic historical records (Paddaya 1995: 114). One can find examples of writings which superficially bear resemblance to the kinds of critical speculations proposed much later in Europe by Rousseau in his 1755 *Discourse on the Origin of Inequality*. Warder (1961: 49) describes Buddhist texts in which early societies were morally perfect, and there was:

> no state or kingship, no sex or marriage, no property, no work, no caste, no war, no old age, or disease ... Afterwards it was discovered that food (rice) could be stored. As soon as this was done there was a shortage of wild rice. The land was then divided into private holdings to ensure fair distribution, but as a result of this theft was invented.

Hindu and Buddhist cosmologies involve almost infinite time-spans, but their very duration makes possible room for histories within such cycles, and a separation of cosmological and human historical events and ages. There is no logical barrier on forms of linear evolutionary histories within the general scheme of things.

The representation of time within south and east Asian cosmologies and frameworks is, however, in contrast to Judaeo-

4. Other traditions

Christian chronologies. These include a dated moment of creation, with cumulative genealogies of Biblical peoples eventually offering the starting point of 4004 BCE as calculated by Bishop Ussher in the mid-seventeenth century. This short chronology puts particular constraints on the production and understanding of difference through time, just as the eighteenth- and nineteenth-century lengthening of initially geological chronologies and understandings of the age of the earth (Porter 1979) enabled new processes of change to be adduced for human history and biological evolution. A short chronology tends to support views of foundational creation of difference, such as unique relationships of chosen people with God, inherently unequal variable racial endowments, or a relatively fast-moving history to explain subsequent differentiation from an original equality. These tensions were important within the nineteenth-century debates between monogenists and polygenists, and Creationists and evolutionists (Stocking 1982; Bieder 1986; Patterson 2001: 7-34).

Rather than encompassing alternation or cyclicity, a Judaeo-Christian view encourages a much more linear sense of both history and life, with what (Eliade 1991: 143) calls a ' "concrete and irreplaceable" time … involving unique events such as incarnation, crucifixion, and redemption'. However, despite this linearity, from the medieval period until the eighteenth century in western Europe, suggests Ferguson (1993), most ideas of history were not progressive, but rather emphasised a general decline during contemporary times, or since Creation, albeit with eventual salvation. Janko (1997) emphasises that, as with other traditions, it is impossible to subsume the preceding but persistently influential Greek and Roman authorities within a single model. Although regenerative cyclicity and overall degeneration are the most common frameworks, even within single authors both pessimism and optimism about the past and future course of human history can be found.

91

There arc also precursors of subsistence-based social evolutionary schemes: Lovejoy and Boas (1965: 93-6) refer to the late fourth-century BCE writings of Dicaearchus with a time of plenty, succeeded by a pastoral and then agricultural life. Book Five of Lucretius's *De Rerum Natura* was also influential on many later writers, with a broadly progressive history in which civilisation was, despite bringing warfare, an advance on man's initial rude state; and Diodorus Siculus, also in the first century BCE wrote of the first men leading a 'wretched existence', without homes, fire or cultivated food. 'Speaking generally, in all things it was necessity itself that became man's teacher', he added (Didorus Siculus 1933: 31; see also Rudebeck 2000: 36-64).

Much later in Britain, for example, the comparative ethnologists who were delineating the lines of progress felt obliged to argue against a continuing idea of degenerationism. Responses to continued industrialisation included William Morris's guild socialism, which looked back to medieval times as inspiration for a less alienated craft form of labour, as well as progressive schemata such as those of Marx and Engels. Dominant frameworks of historical understanding come into being as the result of a combination of culturally-mediated circumstances. Social evolution is a particular conjunction of ways of describing and understanding what we would now call cultural difference, and concepts of the nature and causes of sequences of events. In social evolution these understandings were explicitly directional and often teleological, and gave a particular overall shape to perceptions of history.

Difference and time

All these ways of producing history are about ordering perceived difference: for our purposes here, difference between humans. A typical way of ascribing difference is by a process of subtraction, working from a projection of idealised understandings of the self or the writer's world onto other societies or spheres. These ideals are measured against the perceived Other: pagans are 'us' without proper religion; savages lack aspects of civilisation or culture or intellect; women are males without certain physical or mental capacities. The results of these processes for producing discursive difference are arranged along axes of real or mythical time or space, or in relation to other cultural values.

As a social practice, how such anthropological difference is cognised and constructed is clearly dependent upon which categories are deemed important and relevant in any particular cultural and historical context. Manners and customs including language, religious practices, mode of subsistence, dress or lack of it, and nature of government, as well as physical characteristics and appearances, are used as ways to classify others. Typically, there is a tendency subsequently to use the presence of one trait as a signifier of generalised others – *los Indios*, savages (Berkhofer 1978: 3-49). Such perceived material or behavioural features are also typically linked to other qualities, involving psychological or theological classifications such as Aristotelian natural slaves, gender characteristics and capacities, similarities to animals, or, more recently, spiritual closeness to nature. Thus the fact that 'barbarians' did not speak Greek was also a sign of other incapacities or negative attributes, such as consequent imperfect capacity to form society.

This suggested relationship between language, sociality and other traits had much influence on Spanish attitudes towards New World inhabitants, for example (Pagden 1986: 179-90). It raised issues of biological and psychological continuity and discontinuity – how embracing should the concept of humans (like us) be? For most western Europeans the shock of the new tended to promote initial theses of separateness and discontinuity, which were discarded by some for the Enlightenment doctrine of psychic unity, but then arose again in the context of racial politics, national destiny and the genius of peoples. These axes of distinction are still alive today, but since the Second World War there has been a public as well as scientific tendency to accept a common human nature, but to re-emphasise sometimes allegedly insurmountable or incompatible cultural differences, as in Huntington's (1996) *Clash of Civilizations*, and implicit in much current political rhetoric.

The distinctiveness of the social evolutionary technique of ordering people against a representation of historical time can be seen in comparison with other cultural traditions. In the west, binary distinctions such as that between culture and nature (Glacken 1967; Cosgrove 1993; MacCormack 1980) inform mutually constituting categories such as farmers and foragers, male and female, civilisation and savagery, and west and east respectively. Yet Halbfass (1988: 172) argues that within Hinduism, for example, the internal complexities of religious hierarchy rendered the lowest castes or non-Hindus, although characterised as deviant or impure, irrelevant and unnecessary to self-definition. They were not required as alternative models, or as modes of being against which to reference Hindu identity. From a Brahmin perspective, Hindu categorisation may be considered as 'a sequence of concentric circles, which surround the centre of ritual purity and perfection' (Halbfass 1988: 180). He continues:

Classical Hindu thought has developed ... a complex, internally differentiated framework of orientation, a kind of immanent universe of thought, in which the contrast of the 'indigenous' and the 'foreign', of identity and otherness, seems *a priori* superseded, and which is so comprehensive in itself that it is not conducive to any serious involvement with what is different and apart from it – i.e. the 'other' in its otherness.

Halbfass 1988: 187

4. Other traditions

Eurocentrism and incorporation

There is also a relationship between history, difference and scale: the extent over which spatial and temporal processes can be said to apply. The conjectural social evolutionary histories of the eighteenth century were 'universal' histories because they purported to deal with generalised historical processes. Given *a priori* assumptions about human nature and consequent material and psychological needs, they could be applied to the whole of mankind as a way of explaining differences *within* humankind. The relationship between place and difference, however, was initially uncertain. As we have seen, drawing on much earlier Greek thought there had been a tradition of explaining cultural and psychological difference through climatic variation. Montesquieu, in his influential *The Spirit of the Laws* of 1748, assigned observed differences in government and history in large part to the effects of climate on people's dispositions, such as courage. Temperate zones were seen to be the best, and so he argued that differences in climate were 'the major reason for the weakness of Asia and the strength of Europe, for the liberty of Europe and the servitude of Asia' (Montesquieu 1989: 280). Later in the same century Buffon asserted that difference in the American hemisphere tended to diminish both size and sexual ardour in flora and fauna, including humans. In other frameworks contemporaneous human variation could be explained primarily in theological terms – distinguishing those, for example, who had not been exposed to the Christian revelation, or who had 'moved away' from God – but here too history tended to play a role.

There were similar tendencies elsewhere, and it is easy to select citations which suggest that social evolution was far from wholly radical but rather in part the culmination of a Europe-wide trend towards identifying and separating natural law from divine intervention and Biblical constraints (Hodgen

1964; Slotkin 1965). There was much concern with political organisation demonstrated with the debates surrounding the nature and origins of the social contract; by the late sixteenth century there were proposed technological and even subsistence sequences. Hodgen (1964: 490) writes of the 'supposedly original but actually imitative scholarship of the early Enlightenment'. Classical social evolution really happens with not only the turn to, but also the general acceptance of materialism, rather than theology, among those whom we conceive as our intellectual and disciplinary ancestors; but it is arguably also the secularisation of a particular Christian attitude towards history (cf. Fabian 1983: 3). The cultural conditions for producing universal histories, such as social evolution, comprise three inter-related aspects: identifying certain differences, explaining and evaluating them, and organising and expressing them chronologically.

The onset of comparative ethnography was spurred by the necessity of engaging with 'new' people. The geographical remoteness and enormity of the Americas in particular, coupled with the lack of ancient textual authority, allowed the New World and its inhabitants to become the vessels for all kinds of fantasies and explanations. The recognition of similarities – that it was possible to assimilate those encountered within a vision of humanity – promoted universality outside the bond of revealed religion. The perception of discontinuities enabled and promoted the formation of particularly rigid and bounded categories which were a pre-requisite for stadial schemes. These particular conditions of geographical and cultural rupture were not replicated in southern and eastern Asia.

The initial European categorical choices of subsistence and commerce also tell us much of the cultural preoccupations of those writing the conjectural histories, often economists and lawyers, landowners and improvers. They were men interested in the material conditions of life, work, colonisation and trade.

4. Other traditions

Though complex, the category of 'hunters' was Other to the ideal of the seventeenth- and eighteenth-century European (Pluciennik 2002). Specific attitudes towards the relative merits, ideal locations and characteristics of culture, cultivation and nature coloured attitudes towards and the connotations of 'savage hunters' in particular. Thus modern Europeans have engaged with difference under specific conditions and in a particular way. Linear tropes for time and history existed and progressive interpretations were favoured by changing conditions. That other traditions did not develop or show interest in subsistence-based social evolution (Pluciennik 2004), reinforces the argument that it was the product of a very specific set of circumstances and sense of history. European conjectural historians were using their own and proxy experiences as the marker against which to measure progress and improvement. The sense of a personal journey towards the achievable end of salvation became important as a model of and for secular achievement, collective histories and modern political philosophies.

Complexity, scale and variation

The primary role of comparative analysis has been seen within social evolution as a way of separating the superficial from the fundamental, by insisting on looking for commonalities across cultures. It is presumably this aspect which Tilley (1996: 1) had in mind when he wrote: 'There are no cross-cultural generalizations going beyond either the mundane or the trivial.' To which the riposte might be that it depends on who is doing the asking and what we want to know from ethnography or history. Archaeology can of course be used as a way of positing general lessons or even laws about human capacities and behaviours. This is perhaps most obvious within the field of human evolution, though this is itself highly problematic when characterised as seeking a specific point at which modern humans may be said to emerge. In general, though, archaeology with its uncertain biases and often appalling and minute samples would seem to be less suited to offer plausible answers about human capabilities than contemporary sociology, biology, psychology and ethnography, for example. Archaeology is, by and large, not the past tense of ethnography. What archaeology can offer is comparative material about aspects of past material and social practices throughout human history and across global space: it is very good at elucidating difference, and modern techniques mean that we can talk about synchronicity and co-evality. It is this which enables a new agenda for comparative analysis.

In social evolution the term 'complexity' is applied to societies as an antonym of 'simple'. It means 'more' within some inter-related whole, so that there are additional constitutive elements such as social roles, groups, institutions and settlements, often in an hierarchical relationship, and with the potential for more complicated connections between the different components. In social evolution, it is argued that larger groups or communities necessitate or enable greater division of labour, leading to specialisation or the separation of roles, beyond the generally assumed baseline of gender- and perhaps age-related practices.

Complexity thus encompasses economic, social and political aspects. Economic complexity is often seen to relate to the redistribution of desired goods, typically due to spatial and environmental variability, necessitating exchange of materials of restricted source, as well as encouraging specialised production. Such differentiation of tasks may also lead to social heterogeneity such as specialisation in religious, craft or other roles which may involve ranking as well as a greater number of statuses; managerial requirements involve political complexity through specialised institutions such as bureaucracies, and technologies such as writing. The support of certain specialists and elites promotes the extraction of surplus, and also the need to evoke or maintain authority. This latter is required in order to produce some sort of consensus and acceptance of allegiance beyond the household and family, which is seen as the natural recipient for labour and loyalty and which can be cast in terms of genetic preference (Johnson and Earle 1987). Thus progressive social evolution is partly predicated on increasing scales and levels of conformity: if social cohesion and social identity are to be established and maintained in larger polities, then political and social integration in the form of acceptance of hierarchies and allegiance to institutions is required.

Accepting that this is not a self-evident good, many turn to cost-benefit analysis in answering the question 'why?' Social evolution is seen as a progressive integration which involves the subordination of individual or familial interests to a broader socio-political entity. As has been argued since the eighteenth century, there is a potentially closer relationship between material effort and reward with settled subsistence systems such as agriculture, but also a potentially greater fixity of disparity through permanent assignation to more or less productive land, differential access to other valued resources, and the establishment of hereditary statuses. Complexity is thus often equated to ways of enabling relatively permanent inequalities between persons, groups and classes. Chapman (2003: 191) suggests that research into 'complex' societies 'should begin with factors of production and consumption to determine the nature of inequality and the existence or not of social classes', rather than on particular traits such as fortifications or bureaucracy emblematic of some ill-defined complexity.

Rowlands (1989), while accepting that intra-societal forms of 'social closure and exclusion' have evolved, proposes that our particular narratives of simple to complex which constitute social evolution are part of a modern reaction to contemporary

conditions including a search for a perceived loss of authentic-
ity. 'The meta-narrative of simple to complex is a dominant
ideology that organises the writing of contemporary world prehistory in favour of a modernising ethos and the primacy of the
West' (1989: 36). However, the particular categories chosen to
characterise complexity, especially those associated with the
state, are, unsurprisingly, those which concern writers in their
own society. This was subsequently extended to incorporate
non-western societies: he argues that well-meant attempts to
produce prehistories for other parts of the world have only
succeeded in attributing independent origins for the self-same
traits deemed important – 'food production, the state, literacy'
(1989: 33).

If in recent times western polities have become dominant in
terms of material manipulation and economic, military and
political power, it was these conditions which provided the
setting and perhaps the stimulus for ideas of social evolution.
Those writing from within western Europe could point to
broadly homogeneous practices and forms of organisation 'at
home'. This was not so in the European colonies – Australia, the
Americas – where settlers and explorers were confronted with
cultural dislocation. Yet if we look, for example, at the South
Asian archaeological and historical record, we see all sorts of
co-eval divergence, continuities and inter-relationships between societies at different 'stages'. These would include
'microlithic' foragers, forager traders, tribes, states and empires. A social evolutionary perspective demands that the scale
initially be restricted to societies, precisely so that one is enabled to make comparisons between them and allot each a place
on a pre-existing timescale. But if we broaden our focus, we are
rather discussing inter-dependence, co-existence and cultural
variation. Considering such social geographies at the regional
or supra-regional scale, it become increasingly difficult to dif-
ferentiate variation from societal specialisation: beyond a

certain scale variation can be considered an expression of complexity without overall integration – the coherence demanded of the organic analogy and societal focus.

The emphasis on complexity in restricted features can also be argued to ignore simplification in others such as kinship. A decline in overall cultural and ecological diversity is also a concomitant of increasing complexity and scale in certain societies (cf. Kaplan 1960): it depends where we wish to draw the boundaries around social 'systems'. Since variation comprises of divergences from some assumed or given norm, it is dependent upon how, and how closely, one looks, and of course potentially changes with each trait or category under consideration. Chapman (2003: 196) argues that there is a 'very real danger that we are trying to "fit" our archaeological research on past societies into existing evolutionary typologies, rather than finding out how far past social forms were similar or different from those known in the ethnographic record ... It is the search for the "other" that is one of archaeology's greatest challenges.'

One can certainly imagine a broadly anarchist vision, perhaps today closely associated with a Deep Green viewpoint, of complexity comprising many small, variable and interconnected but non-hierarchical communities. This is the vision of co-operation as the natural basis of human society, and was forcefully articulated by Kropotkin (1902) in specific opposition to the social Darwinian and capitalist ethos of competition. At the large scale, such a picture would correspond to a world system – a far-reaching structure of primarily economic interconnections – but one without permanent centres or peripheries: such variation, it can be argued, does not necessarily have to lead or equate to sustained inequalities. Hierarchy among broadly equivalent polities may be difficult to maintain. In relation to prehistoric groups, Rowley-Conwy (2001: 64) has recently argued: 'There is no directional trend among huntergatherer societies. Numerous examples reveal complexity

101

coming and going frequently as the result of adaptive necessities.' As such it is a focus on variability rather than on directional changes in complexity, for Rowley-Conwy linked primarily to environment and subsistence but with consequent social effects, which better describes the contours of prehistory, at least.

Stages and evolutionary logics

What exactly then is undergoing change in social evolution? Although one must eventually 'ground' theories in persons – in what people do as social beings, both individually and collectively – contemporary social or 'socio-cultural evolution' could more properly be called societal evolution. This is in contrast to earlier formulations in which a selection of discrete cultural traits, collectively comprising Culture in the singular, was the ultimate focus of interest. But these societies are further aggregated or abstracted into types and stages which necessarily subsume differences in history, location, cultural expression and eventually form. The procedure is part of the tension between stages or types, concrete examples and recognised variation, and the translation of categories from one discipline to another with very different data-sets and methodologies. These increasing levels of abstraction are applied as the scale of focus is altered from the specific to the general both across space, from the local or regional to the supra-regional and global, and across time. Social evolution insists as part of its remit that it surveys the whole, whether this is placed in typological, physical or some other representation of time. But given the insistence on directionality, social evolution does not attempt to explain the whole of social life. Those societies or groups which are not perceived to undergo transformation in the expected ways may be judged under-developed, stagnant or conservative, unable to overcome the particular conditions of their environment. Such terms are another example of the ways in which change *per se*, as well as direction, is typically valorised and reflective of modern conditions.

Does the scale of socio-spatial or temporal analysis matter? Smith (2003: 33) argues that since, for history viewed as social evolution, the 'shape and mechanism are universal' and ultimately independent of 'spatial variation and human action', social evolutionists are forced to 'focus on the rise and fall of a handful of societal types, conjoined through their essential determination in the material conditions of existence, despite the wide variability in cultural expressions'. This problem of cultural, spatial and temporal variation is inherent in any form of universal social evolution. The implication of the critique is that any necessary rules or processes become so general as to be facile or unilluminating; the counter-argument that investigations become so particular and specific that they cannot say anything useful about general trends, if such there be, or human nature. The temptation is to take a middle path; this is, of course, what happened with the rejection by neo-evolutionists of unilinear schemes of cultural evolution in favour of multiple, parallel and convergent evolution. Such problems with stadial schemes and categorical types form the fuel for debates about the value and applicability of social evolution in general, and drive the internal debates about definitions of particular stages.

Ethnographically one solution has been to talk about tendencies rather than universal attributes: thus Lee and Daly (1999: 3), discussing modern foragers, write about forms of social organisation being a 'major area of convergence', rather than imputing essential characteristics; similarly Bird-David (1994) proposes face-to-face public sociality as typical of, but not confined to, foragers. However, even if these are found to be useful themes for investigating contemporary societies, archaeologists also face the problem of interpreting situations which are not

103

analogous to contemporary practices – for many non-material or non-biological aspects of life, we simply do not know the parameters of variation in the past. Not only is there the common methodological problem that any particular case may not be subsumed under presumed general laws; there is also the issue that archaeology will not necessarily offer the possibility of an appropriate answer.

Under these circumstances, it is attractive to offer archaeologies of the same, in which modern concerns and features are attributed to past peoples, and variation largely becomes a matter of 'non-essential' symbolic or ritual practices, for example. This is not to deny that we must necessarily tack between similarity and difference in developing understandings of the past and humankind. However, we can see how such choices, the way in which we distinguish between those like us, or not like us, are implicated in other political projects, and become written into evolutionary histories and stages in a particular way. As with interpretations of human origins, social evolutionary stories with seamless lines are about the 'becoming of us'; and perhaps offer a grounding in a common humanity. This undoubtedly has its attractive side, but the problem is who precisely is meant by 'us'.

It is thus in this tension between the particular or local and the general that most discrepancies and debates arise. How far are we entitled to abstract from the specific to adduce a general process of change? What are the implications of variability? Those who are critical of aspects of social evolutionary approaches often focus on the ways in which ethnographically or historically known societies or archaeological sequences do not conform to the stages or ideal types proposed by social evolutionists. For example Yoffee (1993: 64), though primarily discussing the origin of states in south-west Asia, pointed to a tendency common to stadial schemes, the requirement that qualitative social change has to be coherent and simultaneous.

4. Other traditions

Archaeologically this often led to a 'checklist' approach which required that all features be present and identifiable – or that one or two traits come to stand for a typological whole.

This strategy of presumed metonymy has perhaps been most important for archaeology, in its attempt to correlate uncertain or partial data with ethnographic types or stages. Its expression at one extreme was seen with the creation of the 'Neolithic Package' within Europe, in which pottery was often taken to stand for a whole series of economic and social attributes (Pluciennik 1998), but it has also been important in the application of chiefdoms to the archaeological record, for example. Many archaeologists found the concept useful and stimulating in trying to think about societies which seemed intermediate in social and economic complexity between early farming communities and urban civilisations or states, but arguably it rapidly began to constrain the ways in which such societies were conceptualised.

In Yoffee's view archaeological data present a much more varied picture of socio-political institutions and change than is suggested by abstracted stages or types, a point emphasised by Shennan (1993: 58), who argues that the strength of archaeological data is to reconstruct 'specific social practices', not 'generalized social institutions'. Nevertheless Yoffee (1993: 72 and figure 6.6) continues to support a more nuanced and complex version of social evolution, though 'many different evolutionary trajectories can exist and ... not all known human societies fall on the progressive steps of a social evolutionary ladder'. Working with the same material, Smith (2003: 40) makes a similar point more strongly, arguing that social evolutionary approaches necessarily reduce variability 'in order to illustrate a categorical totality such as the Simple Chiefdom or "Archaic State" '. A term such as state 'unifies and gives conceptual coherence to what are in fact a large number of discrete political practices' (Smith 2003: 97). Similar arguments have been made about other definitional terms such as hunter-gatherer in ethnography and archaeology (e.g. Barnard 1983, Bender 1978), or Neolithic in archaeology (Pluciennik 1998), whether explicitly used within social evolutionary schemes or not. Their long and specific histories mean that they have come to be understood within certain schemes of meaning.

What is at stake here is not only the functional value of particular terminologies. In the struggle to articulate ideas it is common to feel that the accretions of meaning, the connotations of existing terms impede what one is trying to say. Some resort to neologisms – writing about small-scale, middle-range or early complex societies, for example. Others attempt to redefine the terms. Smith (2003: 90) notes that already by 1931 political theorists had proposed '145 distinct definitions' of the State; Chapman (2003: 42-3) the increase in proposed types of chiefdoms by archaeologists during the 1970s. Yet others argue that the focus on definition is itself part of the problem, and in line with recent emphasis on the value of relational thinking and agency theory propose that social process is best understood at the local or regional level. This does not have to preclude comparative analysis, but the goal is to elucidate the reasons for difference in historical trajectory, rather than extract common denominators.

All these strategies are reflections of intellectual struggle and genuine commitment to make broader sense of the disparate data of anthropology and archaeology. But each also has implications for contemporary politics. In relation to the origin of the State, for example, Smith (2003: 97) argues that 'studies of early complex polities have been engaged in writing a profound backstory to current politics, one that universalizes and thus legitimizes current political systems by rooting them in a far-off antiquity connected to the present in an unbreakable chain of historical causation'. The nature of socio-political organisation is thus deemed to be the result of an inevitable metahistorical process, rather than one grounded in the here and now and in the practical disposition of authority.

In Smith's view, those espousing change whether from the political 'left' or the 'centre' are equally disabled by social evolution. Classic Marxian programmes based on social evolutionary typologies argue that emancipation will come only through full-scale revolution – the coherent and simultaneous shift demanded by stadial schemes – while social evolution may also place the impetus for change in factors beyond the reach of intended individual or collective action. Either way, argues Smith (2003: 98) 'archaeologies of early complex polities contribute to a crisis of faith in the viability of contemporary political action'. In social evolutionary terms, the contemporary State or, in earlier formulations, 'Civilisation' and its associated practices may be portrayed as inevitable because of the way in which its institutions and political technologies – elites, bureaucracies, writing, taxation, the use of physical force – can be seen as homologous with ours: in the early State or preceding farming 'villages' we recognise, or construct, the familiar (cf. Rowlands 1989: 32).

There are at least two further related questions, the answers to which although apparently empirical are also dependent upon perspective and have political implications. How long is the social evolutionary time scale? Has the tempo of social evolution changed? Since social evolutionists tend to see population pressure as the prime mover, the first stage of social evolution lasts for several tens of thousands of years, from the 'origin' of modern humans until reliance upon agriculture. If it is accepted that anatomically modern humans possessed the same physical and intellectual capacities as we do, the fact that reliance on managed or domesticated crops and/or animals arose independently in different parts of the world relatively late in the human career, about ten thousand years ago, is seen as an enforced change. Although there may be associated proxi-

107

mate causes such as individual invention, or, more commonly today, responses to climatic or environmental changes, the shift towards cultivation is seen as the consequence of the need for subsistence intensification in a world in which population movements were increasingly circumscribed.

The classic recent global statement of this model was given by Cohen (1977), though similar speculative explanations had been offered in the mid-eighteenth century. The subsequent increase in the rate of population growth may be ascribed to various factors including relaxation of physical or cultural constraints on reproduction typical of hunter-gatherers, such as earlier weaning, the benefit gained by additional household labour, and so forth. Populations and communities are thus enabled to grow, and subsequent transformations into chiefdoms and states are provoked by the need to manage and integrate ever larger agglomerations of people, though the first cities, states and empires mark a qualitative shift around five thousand years ago.

The next change in the rate of population growth is seen in modern times with the inception of capitalism, when the combination of industrialisation, agricultural improvement and, crucially, reduced infant mortality rates allowed the explosion in world population which is still continuing. This focuses attention on three key moments: the agricultural, urban and industrial 'revolutions'. Prior to the first human history was largely a matter of geographical expansion but social evolutionary stasis; subsequently inexorable but steady population growth demanded incremental shifts in modes of socio-political organisation and integration eventually leading to the State; finally capitalism provoked the industrial revolution whose consequences are in the process of unfolding today. Thus Sanderson (1995: 389-92) identifies four principal material causal factors – 'demographic, ecological, technological and economic forces' – permutations of which have different saliences within different stages. Pre-State societies including hunter-gatherers are 'deeply conservative', and subsequent agrarian civilisations are characterised by a kind of 'inertia', an echo of Marx's Asian Mode of Production. It is only with capitalism that 'a new evolutionary dynamic was introduced into the world' based on the logic of capital accumulation which drives exponential growth and change (Sanderson 1995: 392; 2002).

These kinds of reading suggest that social evolutionary time is accelerating, and may even be used to propose that different eras show different evolutionary logics. However, as Rowlands (1989: 32-3) notes, for evolutionary archaeologists 'historical sequences that lack all or most of the features that define complexity become "problematic" in the sense that they cannot be placed on any sort of evolutionary continuum'. Just like Clarke's (1980) *Mesolithic Prelude*, periods and places without change in the chosen categories become invested at best with the quality of marking time. This is saying more than that there are potentially different combinations and changes in the importance of basic factors. Further, these vary not by societies as such, but rather by stages or broad ethnographic categories. Suggesting that we can identify social evolution over increasingly shorter periods the closer societies get to 'our' time and to becoming like 'us' is a familiar strategy from recent politics; it can deny effective past participation in human history to many prehistoric groups or their supposed modern representatives, who thereby only have quaint or exotic traditions, or in any event no meaningful, that is directional, change.

5

The frameworks of social evolution

Having described some of the forms which social evolution has taken, is it possible to offer a definition of what must constitute any such theory? At its weakest, we might suggest that it comprises any recognition of difference and associated explanation of its genesis. However, this would then include all those precursors from at least Classical Greece onwards: the argument would then be that any scheme, whatever the underlying philosophies, utilising anthropological distinctions between people placed in some relation to time, would qualify. This is a plausible case, just as the idea of progress can be 'traced' backwards, and Stoczkowski (2002) has argued that ideas about human origins show impressive persistence.

A stronger argument can be made that social evolution is 'any structural transformation in a sociocultural system' (Sanderson 1990: 154), but this already depends on identifying what comprises the important aspect – social structure or organisation, rather than other axes of potential variation – and also assumes that it is possible and meaningful to identify sometimes contiguous and co-eval societies as separate systems. But boundaries are always porous in space and time, and people, genes, ideas and material goods flow across them. Further, ideas and modes of boundedness are not static. Notions and practices of territoriality, identity and membership of 'societies' are variable; social geographies can be mapped in many ways depending on how we want to characterise such flows. On the continental scale, we have continuously varying landscapes of social processes, which societal evolution is just one way of selecting from and ordering.

Social evolution involves, then, a particular sociological perspective, which is again a component of modern, that is, post-Enlightenment disciplinary perspectives (see Barnard 1999 for a genealogy of concepts of hunter-gatherer *societies*; cf. Rowlands 1989: 35 for other disciplines). Nevertheless, bearing all the above qualifications in mind, we can utilise Sanderson's definition of social evolution: 'the provision of a general mechanism or set of mechanisms to account for ... general directional sequences of societal change' (1990: 9; see also 1995: 381-402). The key issue here is 'directionality'. Evolution, as we have seen, is sometimes opposed to history, in the sense that it is argued not only that there is a long-term pattern, but also that such a pattern must be grounded in more than chance events or contingency.

However, there is clearly a difference here between social and biological evolution. Although both are historical in that they describe and explain change over time, the latter is about identifying the process which enables Darwin's 'descent with modification'. Measured against a notion of adaptedness, there is nothing to say that complexity will *necessarily* be the result, although it can be argued that diversification within ultimately constrained environments tends towards more complex ecosystems. Social evolution, though, generally claims more: it proposes that whatever the role of contingency, there is a shape to history, a directionality which whether in a strong or weak sense means more than description of sequence and mechanism: there is an overall *process* of qualitative, and not just cumulative change. Dealing with one biological species, whatever the rhetorical devices which have been used to place other contemporary 'less developed' societies in *our* past, it has long

111

been recognised that all of us as social and biological persons can draw upon equally lengthy histories. Fabian (1983) suggests that the radical implications of this practical co-evality, in which 'we' and 'they' do not merely exist within the same physical time but engage as co-present actors, were not dealt with by ethnographers. He argues that many epistemological, literary and political strategies were developed which sustain or re-introduce the valuation of societies or culture according to their place in social evolutionary time.

Much comparative ethnography and social evolutionary archaeology can be said to deny certain societies or cultures history in another sense, by equating history with change. Service, for example, discussing precisely this question, pointed to the Arunta people of Australia. 'Certainly aboriginal Arunta culture is not younger than Western civilization [i.e. with a 'shorter' history]; it is obviously a great deal older, and precisely therein lies one of the virtues of studying that culture' (1971: 7). He continues: 'What else can explain such a culture, then, but that there have been survivals into the present of ancient cultural forms which because of relative isolation have maintained a relatively stable adaptation'. Since soon after Service wrote many efforts have been made to show that all societies have meaningful histories, whether or not we equate them with change, and by using methods other than written texts (e.g. Wolf 1982, Leacock and Lee 1982, Bender & Morris 1988). But of course social evolution depends precisely upon recognising directional change as opposed to 'just' variation.

If we accept that all societies, whatever their characteristics, are equally evolved at any given point in time, it raises questions about the ways in which social evolutionary narratives are put together, and makes it clear that ranking societies by any means, including time, is always an evaluative judgement. The implications of ranking co-existing societies as though they represent, however imperfectly, former conditions have been far-reaching. In recent years within anthropology the most forceful critique has been offered by Fabian. He insists that the 'scandal' of what he calls allochronism permeates anthropology up to the present, but has been particularly prevalent within social evolutionary frameworks which make difference purely the result of 'natural' laws operating over time (Fabian 1983: 147).

Even if we set aside the ways in which social evolution has been and is used to judge contemporaneous societies and yet place them temporally in relation to the author's present, what might this mean if we looked solely at archaeological evidence? Taking approximately synchronous surveys across the globe or some smaller regions, we would clearly generally find 'societies' exhibiting very different sizes, extents and forms of socio-political and economic organisation as well as less obviously functional forms of cultural expression. It is only since modern times that we can legitimately deem all societies to be interconnected and variously subject to or agents of encapsulation, domination and inter-penetration, and empirically sharing not only the same space, but also the same time in more than a purely physical sense. Before that, one might argue, it makes little sense to talk of social evolution in the singular except in the most generalised sense. This does not make social evolution 'wrong', but it may often be either inappropriate or inadequate, both as a framework for ethnography, and for much archaeology, depending on what questions we wish to ask.

The argument against this, of course, is that there are sufficient examples of parallel and convergent evolution (say, from Asia and Meso-America in relation to state formation) to be able to perform the final abstraction. The differences, argue proponents of a generalised social evolution, are either epiphenomenal or the results of localised conditions: say, restrictions on growth or the constraints of environmental possibilism. The key point about social evolution is to identify *necessarily* shared processes and outcomes, by virtue of our human needs and capacities.

But proceeding in this way equally necessarily downplays the importance of different ways of being and reduces all histories to one. If we accept that 'culture' is not the froth on the materialist infrastructure, but rather permeates and informs every aspect of being and practice, then variation must be considered not as the surface of the real history but as part of the essence of human histories. Rather than being inclusive by virtue of bringing the whole human race under one umbrella, social evolution often unwittingly denies other histories and other possibilities. By working within an all-embracing paradigm even those who are suspicious of either the fact or the nature of 'progress' but wish to use knowledge of the past as a springboard for a better future, may be misreading the political implications of social evolution.

The politics of social evolution

The insistence on a particular view of directionality has many important implications. Social evolutionary views have generally been closely linked to an idea – many would say an ideology – of progress. There are strong reasons for associating stadial social evolution with modernity and particular forms of capitalism. This form of economic organisation expresses a logic predicated on the necessity of growth, and can consequently be characterised as both expansive and predatory whether within particular societies or beyond, in the forms of colonialism, imperialism and in aspects of globalisation (cf. Patterson 1997).

Those who have been responsible for the texts discussed in this book, including myself, as members of wealthy, western elites have been the beneficiaries of the results of this system. As such, it is easy to see how for those apparently looking out, from the inside; or down, from the top; or back, from the modern present, the contours of cultural and historical difference seem to make sense in a particular way. And it is clear that the ways in which people describe trajectories are heavily dependent not only on personal convictions but also on socio-cultural contexts. These then enable authors such as Trigger (1989) to characterise wider currents of optimism and pessimism, albeit among particular classes and societies, which inflect the predominant views of historical change.

Yet there have always been critics of, and dissenters from, progressive social evolution too: the idea of degeneration, whether founded in Biblical exegesis and theology, or types of romanticism borne out of a sense of alienation from feelings or nature; philosophies of history involving cyclical rise and fall or even stasis; or political claims related to emancipation: that whatever the lessons of the past, human conditions could be ameliorated and 'real' progress attained, that is, in the direction desired by the author.

Does social evolution necessarily entail progress? This is not quite as simple a question as it may seem at first glance. The sense of progress has usually been meant in two ways, though often conflated: firstly, as the succession of necessary steps towards some pre-ordained, predictable and valued goal. The second sense refers to cumulative empirical change in technological capacities, or the scale and scope of trade and exchange, for example, which may engender qualitative changes in social organisation such as the extent of political and economic control.

The first sense, involving an overall *telos* of history in which a pre-ordained end was immanent in the human condition, may seem a very nineteenth-century or earlier viewpoint, redolent of a theological sense of divine or human mission or Hegel's World Spirit. But clearly this could be and was recast in a secular mode from the Enlightenment onwards, expressed in the disciplinary search for social scientific laws of change which

115

was one of the aims of Tylor for a general 'science of man', and of many others since. One of the consequences has been to use the study of social evolution to justify the study of archaeology more generally as a discipline of contemporary relevance and an important aid in mapping or even shaping the future.

The second sense of progress is involved in judgements about whether empirically-recorded changes can be viewed individually or collectively as improvements, itself a term very much associated with the ideology and practices of capitalism. As we have seen, the concept is often entangled with discussion of the relationship between Culture and cultures, or between general and specific evolution. However, individually and contextually, it can make sense to talk about progress in relation to some pre-defined yardstick. It is perfectly reasonable to point to progress in technology, understood, say, as the increased ability to manipulate material, whether the outcomes are perceived as best characterised by good, as in medical treatments, or bad, as in capacity for warfare. Thus even those who wish to argue that social evolution as a fact is far from an unmitigated good, identify progress in the sense of intensification, greater integration or technological achievement, even though they may deem it an unfortunate direction.

Most of the recent literature still falls within a broadly progressive framework. Johnson & Earle (1987: 15) stated simply: 'We see the evolutionary process as an upwards spiral', meaning an iterative process of intensification, but often the idea of progress is more implicit or qualified. One common image is that of an undulating line which, despite local falls, shows an overall upward trend. Thus Childe, writing in 1941, concluded that 'Progress is real if discontinuous.' He continued: 'The upward curve resolves itself into a series of troughs and crests. But ... no trough ever declines to the low level of the preceding one; each crest out-tops its last precursor' (1964: 292).

5. The frameworks of social evolution

Of what does that progress consist? Archaeologically, it has a long history in relation to technology, meaning not only absolute control over material, but also and especially the ability to distance oneself from dependence on the natural environment. It is this perception which is at the heart of concepts of the neolithic step forward. But it is certainly not self-evident that the occurrence of extensive famines and other often anthropogenically-induced disasters is necessarily outweighed by the benefits of reliance on agriculture. This involves a judgement from a specific position about the relative merits of a particular and 'fundamentally unstable' way of life (Harlan 1995: 115). Although agriculture certainly does enable larger and more concentrated populations, and consequent forms of specialisation and their material expression, there are many costs involved including decreased biodiversity, the simplification of ecosystems and consequent lack of resilience, and the extension of risk to ever larger populations. This is not necessarily to demand a return to self-sufficiency and sustainability, but rather to suggest how all evaluations in relation to progress are culturally-mediated.

Nowadays the concept of progress is often reserved for increasing social complexity. For example Carneiro (2003: 129-30, 282) refers back to Spencer and reserves the term evolution only for what he sees as instances of the process of 'aggregation and integration', for societies on an 'ascending trajectory' and displaying 'increasing complexity' while overall 'advances are intermingled with retreats, peaks alternate with troughs'. Thus the transformation or fall of the Roman, Minoan or Harappan polities is, for Carneiro, devolution. But this is a prime example of selecting only change in particular forms of political and ideological integration as evidence of advance, at the expense of other forms of organisation and inter-relationship. Though with a long pedigree, the idea that evolution does not necessarily represent a steady advance perhaps became

117

more common with the decline of unilinear models in favour of convergent and parallel evolutionary schemes, and also with those seeking explanations for the 'collapse' of complex societies (Tainter 1988). However, we can also point to much more explicit rejections of the fact of progress. These too seem to have become more frequent in recent years, as a sign of uncertainty, if not outright pessimism about contemporary trends. As such, they seem to be very much rooted in immediate concerns, though the responses are not necessarily simple.

Some have championed materialist social evolution as a counter to the excesses of postmodernism, usually glossed as a form of exclusive concern with local interpretation and representation, the undecidability of meaning, a denial of the relevance of material conditions, and a consequent descent into a disabling relativism (e.g. Harris 1979; Trigger 1995, 1998; Carneiro 2003). The concern is with the dismissal of social evolution 'merely' as ethno- and Eurocentric ideology – as representation. 'I merely ask all those who fear the onset of a new dark age to join together to strengthen the barriers against mystification and obscurantism in contemporary social science' (Harris 1979: xii).

If 'postmodernists' are said to reject social evolution for what it means, from the Marxist left has come strong criticism of aspects of postmodernism for the denial of the possibility of an emancipatory politics, and trenchant criticism of an allegedly progressive social evolution too. The anthropologist Diamond (1974: 40) wrote of the 'faith in progress' as the 'dominant idea of Western civilization':

> Caught in the contradictions of society, Westerners see themselves as ciphers of history; incomplete and always waiting to be completed. Disintegrated by the extreme division of labour, by competition for goods and services and status rivalries, they obsessively anticipate integra-

tion. The idea of progress is, above all, the precipitant of unresolved social and personal conflicts in modern civilization ... It is the awareness of this conflict, along with the effort at resolving it that creates the sense of unresolved movement towards specific goals which are defined as progressive.

Hence for Diamond, the recuperation of the idea of progress must be inspired by non-western societies in which individual fulfilment is the measure of success. 'The real issue is qualitative: it concerns participation in a culture, the personal command of cultural possibilities.'

Harris too referred to the 'indoctrination' of the idea of progress. Although admitting improvements for many over the last century, he argues that 'much of what we think of as contemporary progress is actually a regaining of standards that were widely enjoyed during prehistoric times' (Harris 1979: 8). Noting increasing pollution and other industrial problems he suggests that western culture is, like others in the past, reaching the limits of growth. Over a shorter time-scale Wallerstein (1983) also challenges acceptance of the fact of progress present in both liberal and marxist thought. Material progress has largely been confined to the few: rather, he argues, 'immiseration' has been geographically dispersed (cf. Sanderson 1995). One does not have to adopt a form of quantitative utilitarianism to argue that the sum of human unhappiness has increased. Ecological impacts and consumption imbalances also make it highly dubious to be able to talk in any simple terms about progress in the sense of improvement. Evolutionary histories – the outcomes and impacts of social evolution – could also be written from non-anthropocentric viewpoints. Kintz (2001) makes an impassioned plea that archaeologists must decide whether to continue to collaborate with the expansionist and destructive practices of modern capitalism, or align themselves with environmentalists who believe that responsibility should rather be towards 'Mother Earth' (Fig. 6).

Academically, then, there are many who reject the idea of moral, cultural, material or political progress as a necessary adjunct to social evolution. In the broader intellectual sphere Williams (1975: 18-22) shows how over a shorter timescale many within the heart of the progressing modern west responded to change through forms of nostalgia, even if they did not subscribe fully to the idea of a once Golden Age. Many today are attracted by the idea of lost knowledges, histories which place the Fall in the shift from matriarchies to patriarchies, or understand social evolution as a narrative of spiritual decline. These readings compete with those conditioned by *laissez faire* liberalism and the idea that history is on 'our' side – that social evolution is a positive record of inexorable and inevitable change.

One's perspective on social evolution has relevance to current conditions described as globalisation, the increasing inter-penetration of the cultural, economic and political on a global scale. While some have argued that this internationalisation and other recent trends suggest less socio-cultural and socio-economic diversity and more homogeneity, others have pointed to the phenomenon of 'glocalisation' – the production and increased awareness and salience of difference and various forms of identity politics, for example. Few social evolutionists have predicted possible futures (though see Sanderson 1995: 358-80), but even in the relatively short term we can at least envisage new geopolitical alliances emerging, the sites of economic and cultural hegemony shifting, and the decline of nation-states in favour of new forms of supra-national political and economic organisation and institutions – or collapse and re-formation. There are at least plausible scenarios which suggest that in this sense, at minimum, change has not stopped – we are not at the 'End of History'. The production of narratives

Fig. 6. *Civic Venom,* published in Hull, England, in the early 1980s: an example of the Deep Green perspective.

which lead inexorably to modern capitalist nation-states involves the construction of a *necessary* trajectory from *contingent* processes, and from a very particular chronocentric and geopolitical viewpoint.

For those on the liberal left the value of studying social evolution and archaeology is because knowledge is the key to emancipation and future change. 'To change social life for the better, one must begin with the knowledge of why it usually changes for the worse' (Harris 1978: 11; cf. Trigger 1998: 261-3; Chapman 2003: 196-8; Smith 2003). This notion that archaeology can act as a social good is attractive, not least for those with present-day political concerns seeking to justify a discipline which can easily be accused of irrelevance or dilettantism. It becomes a way of reclaiming effective political agency in the face of increasingly distant and difficult to challenge institutions and structures.

There are sometimes tensions here: since social evolution is both directional and predicated upon cross-cultural regularities and pan-human characteristics, it is difficult to see why agency directed towards social justice should be more efficacious in the present or future than in the past. If we are at the mercy of structural conditions and evolutionary logics then pointing to the past may offer little more than the opportunity to say 'I told you so'. Indeed, although Sanderson argues that social evolution is a form of historical analysis, he also problematically suggests, despite his rejection of developmentalist or teleological perspectives, that 'if we started social evolution over again we would get very similar results' (1995: 386-7), that is, that while the overall form and structure of societies are in some sense determined, specific 'historical' events are not. Alternatively, if our argument is against exploitation, repression and inequality of treatment of people and other species, then it is hard to see why we should need archaeology to tell us of the fact rather than contemporary analysis. The value of archaeology and anthropology may rather be in generally widening each of our horizons about the possible, through offering a wider and more fulfilling perspective, and engagement with all kinds of alterity.

Rowlands (1989: 37-9) has discussed three possible political responses to social evolution *qua* a narrative of simple to complex. An insistence on resistance through local and localised knowledges, he argues, is simply an inversion of the dominant form which ultimately reproduces it. A second strategy of a radical difference and anarchist relativism so that 'all pasts are essentially incomparable and unique' may enable the dominated to claim a unique identity, but typically the already powerful elite can, among other strategies of dominance, claim and use science as 'independent access to truth and knowledge' (1989: 38). What is rather needed is the 'return of a confidence in the Enlightenment project of a human liberation being achieved through the rational understanding of our worlds'. The duty of archaeology is to 'investigate the characterization of difference and the ordering principles of past social totalities by avoiding the conditions which constitute them as characteristic only of the present' (Rowlands 1989: 39).

Rather than treating archaeological and ethno-historical materials as a source for a single meta-narrative, however it is valued, one could perhaps use them rather as a source of emancipatory alternatives. Not in the sense of a Romantic or nostalgic return, nor as a warning about what necessarily happened in the long-run, but rather to present alternative histories precisely to show that just as pasts were different, so too can be futures. The idea of progress does not have to be seen as a necessary concomitant of emancipation, understood as the possibility of change for the better. Such political intentions and activism can be considered on a timescale more appropriate for human action, agency and engagement. Ideas of local or relative improvement are not necessarily opposed to broader

123

philosophies of cycles or even degeneration in human history. Archaeologies and histories cannot be models of, but they can be models for the *possibility* of present and future actions.

Social evolution in practice

The content of social evolution as traditions of thought, disciplinary and educational practices and terminologies can structure thinking even when not explicitly addresssing social evolution. The most persistent division in archaeological and ethnographic practice and intellectual labour has been that between foragers and farmers. Zvelebil (1996b) has written about how contemporary national and supra-national identities, usually predicated upon combinations of cultural, territorial and biological persistence (*'Blut und Boden'*) rarely draw upon any notion of hunter-gatherer ancestry, although in principle for some societies this would enable even greater longevity to be claimed. Zvelebil (1996b: 146-7) argues that this is because the visibility of farming, colonial and imperial encounters with foraging 'savages', and idealisation of a particular type of rural landscape fed into national identities which saw peasant farmers as 'harbingers of true national culture and character'. It is worth noting that for many contemporary indigenous groups, encapsulated within or in opposition to nation-states, rights not only to land but also particularly to engage in traditional hunting and fishing are, however, crucial parts of cultural identity and political activism.

Archaeologically the Neolithic is often glossed as sedentary and agropastoral, which is itself a particular form of western farming, and uniquely with the potential for social and economic complexity. It is commonly equated to a radical upwards step in human history. The arrival of agriculture represents a 'new way of life, as well as a totally new relationship with the environment ... a dramatic shift in the trajectory of cultural evolution' (Gebauer & Price 1992: 1). Clark (1980: 7) called his brief and positive overview of early Holocene foragers in Europe *Mesolithic Prelude*, suggesting that the importance of the period lay in the fact that it constituted 'an essential prelude to fundamental advances in the development of culture', namely, the Neolithic. Arias (1999: 404) suggests that investigating the transition to farming 'confronts questions fundamental to the understanding of humanity'. For Price (2000: 1) the agricultural transition was 'arguably the most important event in human prehistory ... that sets the stage for most of the significant subsequent developments in human society', and for Mazurié de Keroualin (2003: 5) a 'decisive step in human history'.

One of the implications of such stadial consensus has been the negative consequences for perceptions of 'hunter-gatherers', which category name itself reflects a complex history. In the eighteenth century 'hunters' were equated to savages: the latter, according to Pagden (1993: 14), given a modern sense by Montesquieu and Rousseau and meaning pre-social beings 'at the beginning of human social time'. Much later 'hunter-gatherers' was introduced as a fairer representation of subsistence activity, though it has been argued that the hyphenated order of hunter-gatherer reproduces a specifically male ideology by privileging the first over the second 'female' term, even while reversing the typical dietary importance of the two activities. But it is still foragers and pastoralists, the first two steps on the eighteenth-century social evolutionary ladder, who are commonly referred to and defined by their presumed subsistence mode.

The archaeological origins and spread of agriculture are seen as fundamental to the modern world, and for that reason have attracted much academic attention. Since the 1920s much research has focused on identifying the primary centres of domestication. Attention focused on south-west Asian agropastoralism and Meso-American maize, beans and squash. This was reinforced by the fact that many of these plants and animals can be morphologically and now genetically recognised as domesticated, unlike tubers or many tree crops of South America, Asia, Africa and the Pacific. Nevertheless the number of 'core areas' with early cultivation or domestication has now expanded from three to perhaps eight (south-west Asia, Meso-America, Andean South America, north and south China, Papua New Guinea, sub-Saharan Africa and the eastern United States), although there are many other areas where plant and animal management occurred in prehistory. These too show evidence of the sorts of processes identified with agricultural origins, such as Europe for dog; central and northern Asia for horse and reindeer; and south-east Asia, Australia and parts of Africa for root crops.

All this challenges the traditional adherence to identifying core areas for the origins of agriculture as the key question. It also raises doubts about generalised explanations that environmental changes, population pressure or the intentional avoidance of uncertainty in subsistence may be considered as the prime mover for either agricultural emergence (e.g. Smith 1994) or the adoption and spread of farming. The long delays in the adoption of certain domesticated crops as a subsistence mainstay in much of Eurasia and in eastern North America, among other places, suggest that this explanation is insufficient. The distinctions made between centres and non-centres of agricultural innovation look increasingly shaky, unless we accept that our interest is in large part conditioned by the accidents of genetic contingency and the current dominance of certain staple crops (Pluciennik & Zvelebil 2003).

Until recently the archaeology of agricultural origins and spread has been a clear example in which what leads to 'us' is seen as a more important and interesting question than other pathways or histories, which could be considered equally stimulating and suggestive. Rowlands (1989: 33) indeed argues that the Enlightenment and Childean view of the origins of agriculture as a liberation from the tyranny and vagaries of the natural environment is itself a particular 'modern Western disposition'. Even though definitions of the Neolithic have come under attack in its homeland during recent decades (e.g. Armit & Finlayson 1992; Thomas 1993; Whittle 1996: 4-9; Pluciennik 1998), these criticisms often reproduce or reintroduce the dichotomy albeit in other terms. As such, the Neolithic has been used to mean minimally 'the transition to farming', or to cover everything from cultural *bricolage* (Thomas 1996) to the process of human 'domestication' (Hodder 1990) and a host of variable socio-cultural processes. Yet as Tringham (2000: 22) says:

> It seems amazing that after all these decades we are still allowing the heuristic device of the Three-Age System to direct our interpretational modelling, but it is a truism that the definition of 'Neolithisation' depends a great deal on the criteria used to define 'the Neolithic'.

For example, in a series of papers Zvelebil (1996a, 1998) has explored the parameters of change and social processes in the Baltic region of Europe over the last ten thousand years or so. His primary interest has been the transition to farming, a process which can be said to begin around 4000 BCE and finish around 1500 CE. In northern Europe, the presence of farming communities is recognised archaeologically as reaching the north European plain by around 5000 BCE (Bogucki 2000). But then the spread of farming in this mode appears to halt for more than a thousand years. Only after that does it resume, apparently swiftly in parts of southern Scandinavia, but much more slowly and locally nuanced elsewhere in the region. This 'transition to farming', however, is preceded by archaeologically demonstrable contacts between the two types of society, and with many other implications. Parts of this area show shifts back and forth between agricultural and non-agricultural or pastoral regimes.

Zvelebil suggests that among the archaeologically-interpretable interactions are those of exchange, emulation, hypergyny (the relative 'loss' of women as marriage partners from one adjacent group to another), social competition and conflict. He has also suggested (1997) that it may be possible to identify the long-term duration, over perhaps ten thousand years, of structures of cosmological thought among certain groups in the area of north-east Europe and Siberia. This shows we do not just have to consider the very local as the bedrock of specificity: rather we can consider local expressions of such cosmologies either as showing common root(s), or as demonstrating the maintenance and mutual influence of inter-societal relationships across much of northern Eurasia, a world system of a particular sort. Thus although Zvelebil's social archaeology of the region is characterised by and in tandem with all kinds of short-term, long-term, rapid and slow material and social transformations in various groups around the Baltic area, all these processes are described in terms of a subsistence trajectory. This includes cultures which have been defined as pertaining to a 'transitional' phase. That is, their members are neither fully foragers nor farmers in subsistence, material culture or social organisation or ideology, but persist in an apparently stable state for towards two millennia and hence, as Zvelebil (1998: 23) accepts, 'remain suspended between our traditional notions of the Mesolithic and Neolithic'.

Zvelebil's work is one of the richest and socially-nuanced interpretations currently available for this period. However, it is clearly written within an ultimately social evolutionary framework, explicitly addressing one of the key questions, the shift from one stage to the next; and it uses those often dichotomous terminologies and draws on ethnographies themselves structured within those pre-judged categories of forager and farmer. We do not lose anything by considering this material as a series of regional trajectories rather than a single social evolutionary stadial transition. Rather, doing so may draw our attention to other themes and perspectives. Rowley-Conwy (2001: 62) has suggested we may learn from the example of Jomon foragers in Japan: 'Eight thousand years of complexity did not lead to an indigenous Jomon agriculture. Jomon studies have freed themselves from this predestination, so groups can be examined for their own sake – not for what they might become.'

Perlès' (2001) review of neolithic Greece might be considered a further example of the subtle influence of social evolutionary thought. In an excellent review and discussion of the data, Perlès argues for differentiation and variability among early neolithic communities. She proposes that they were indeed 'complex' societies though not in the social evolutionary sense of hierarchically-organised groups; rather she refers to heterarchical social and economic organisation, 'a form of complexity that we can hardly apprehend, for lack of reference models' (Perlès 2001: 305). Yet Kotsakis (2002) has suggested that the whole premise of the book rests on a modernist preoccupation with origins. It utilises singular and homogeneous categories which rest on the identification of 'mesolithic' and 'neolithic' traditions. Yet, argues Kotsakis (2002: 375), 'The quest for origins is no longer illuminating as soon as the teleological process has neither distinct actors nor a definable end.' Rather than attempt to recover a 'fixity of meaning' for the Neolithic by placing its source in colonisers from Anatolia or the Near East, Kotsakis suggests one could investigate the ambiguous nature of (dis)continuities and the fluidity of cultures and identities.

The structure of all such narratives derives ultimately from Enlightenment categories, most obviously with the divide between hunter-gatherers and farmers as later translated into archaeology. These and many other texts thus continue to emphasise the importance of radical change within a stadial scheme, arguably at the expense of alternative interpretations which would focus on overlapping continuities or shifts in practices which do not coincide with archaeological periodisations or anthropological categories. Even though there are undoubted discontinuities in the archaeological record, these may be partly a function of preconceptions about what we are looking for and the techniques and strategies used: both Pluciennik (1997: 136-7) and Skeates (2003: 173) have even suggested that this may be the case with radiocarbon dating samples related to the Mesolithic-Neolithic transition in Italy, for example. A further implication of stadial schemes is that by highlighting particular horizons of change, the converse – the maintenance of apparent socio-cultural and economic stability which may characterise societies for much longer time-spans – is downgraded in importance as an object of study. This preference for examining change may also be attributed to a particular modern mindset which extends perceptions of current conditions in which flux is the natural condition of existence to the whole of human history. In Childean terms, the climbs towards the 'peaks' are valorised as of more interest and relevance than the troughs or plateaux. Archaeologists have been prone to seek or preferentially value examples of change, of altered subsistence, settlement patterns, social organisation and technology, rather than being equally interested in the apparent maintenance of tradition and stability of practices and material culture. And again this bolsters the framework of a stadial social evolution, in which periods of transition are seen to tell us more, to be more important, than what lies either side of the divide or rupture.

To different degrees and in different ways, the above cases are subtle examples of the retrospective fallacy – the tendency to write anachronistic histories in a particular way, tense and perspective not because we know what eventually happened, but on the assumption that it is obvious 'where' these societies were heading. The issue is recognised as a major problem especially for those engaged with histories of ideas: hindsight can promote the search for putative embryonic versions, the first expressions or the absolute origins only of those ideas or methods which are currently important to us. While such genealogies are part of writing histories, they can also lead to the reification of disembodied ideas, distorted lineages, claims only to particular intellectual ancestors and misreadings or denial of the social contexts and intended meanings in the past. In a similar way social evolution, by defining in advance the direction and stages to which socio-historic processes move and societies ought to aspire, can act to close down the way in which archaeologies are written, and the themes which are judged relevant and important. By focusing on what we know, or think we know, about the directionality and even the 'intentions' of societies to move from one state or stage to another, we already constrain our questions and answers.

We can perhaps ask other questions about transformation and change if we retreat from subsistence and social complexity as the measure of all things. If, as is surely accepted by all anthropologists and archaeologists, all societies are equally capable of change, then the circumstances under which some have changed in particular ways, and others not, are matters of historical contingency and circumstance. Yet the legacy of social evolution still pushes us in the direction of valuing certain sorts of societies in particular ways. This does not necessarily show the invalidity of particular theories or stories about the past, but rather how ingrained certain categories of thought have become, and their often unintended consequences. Neither does it imply that we cannot or should not compare regional sequences and the reasons why they differ. But there is a difficult balance to be struck between global histories –

131

world archaeologies – especially as we might want, politically, to speak about *one* human race; and valorising certain regions or groups which appear to have had 'more history' than others, and which seem to suggest what conditions may be like for all of us in the future.

Anthropology and archaeology are generally too pluralist in content, too diverse in their regional contexts and traditions, and too dependent on data usually produced through unrepeatable exercises such as ethnographic fieldwork and archaeological excavation to make law-like generalisation a useful approach at the local scale. As Flannery (1999) has suggested, useful social evolutionary laws may be impossible: archaeologists tend rather to produce 'historical narrative explanations' (and see Pluciennik 1999). Many archaeological and more broadly socio-cultural statements are under-determined by the data: we can interpret empirical material in many different ways, depending on our interests and the context within which we view it. But while general versus specific evolution, or evolution versus history, are often portrayed as dichotomies or at different ends of a spectrum, they are not mutually exclusive. They are rather part of constellation of approaches which bring different aspects of human histories into focus. In many ways there is an inherent but productive tension between the specific and the general, event and process, history and evolution which is part of any comparative project, part of Wylie's (1989) tacking back and forth between alternative perspectives.

Conclusion

In this book I have necessarily simplified a complex picture and emphasised critical aspects of social evolution as a deliberate counter to the weight of existing literature and cultural understandings. I have not addressed that 'other' evolution, present in socio-biology, evolutionary psychology and neo-Darwinian approaches within archaeology, which would require another book. The aim has been to delineate not only the history of an idea, but also its ramifications and implications for archaeology and anthropology. Academic disciplines cannot be treated in isolation from the rest of the world, whatever the rhetorical accusations about ivory towers. This is because not only are the practitioners of such disciplines and the institutions enabling them engaged in studying the world, they are also of course an important part of it, as sites, agents and instigators of education, research, and intellectual and political debate, as well as being enmeshed within governmental policies. It is often argued that the growth in scale of entities, and the consequent relative impotence of individuals and small groups in the modern world has led to a focus on difference as a way of apparently empowering individuals and smaller groups who may feel 'marginalised', including academics; certainly part of intellectual activity is to react against established norms. Within academia, those interested in the broad picture of socio-cultural evolution have produced a counter-reaction and encouraged others to focus on particularity and difference.

Debates over social evolution are responses to different visions of what constitutes meaningful history. Arguments over what is the best locus for understanding human change, or which aspects of analysis should be prioritised, are at the heart of competing views of human nature and the human condition, especially perhaps about the extent and nature of agency (Dobres & Robb 2000). A generalising concept such as social evolution, by positing metahistorical or transhistorical trends, must rely on structures and processes ultimately or largely outside the control of individual or even collective actors. When these processes are seen as generally benign, or represent partial values uncritically universalised, the tendency is to equate social evolution and progress. When they are seen as against majority interests, not only by definition are the general processes seen as regressive, but there is often an attempt to reclaim agency in the sense of the necessity for political activism. The path of social evolution is seen as a warning.

The historical and comparative approach taken in this book assumes that philosophies of history, whatever their claims to characterise the broad sweep of the past, are also inevitably of their time and place, and with implications for the present and future. Social evolution in its modern form was a strategy invented in the eighteenth century as a particular form of comparative analysis which enabled the incorporation of many forms of alterity into one representation of history and of time. As such it was related to the practices of capitalism, colonialism, imperialism, racism and associated projects including the formation of the modern disciplines of anthropology and archaeology. The view taken here is that while there are and have been other traditions, by the mid-eighteenth century within western Europe there was a coalescence of particular trends and specific features. These were expressed through a materialist and secular philosophy of history with an explicit claim to universality, basically encompassing the same spatial and ethnographic referents of the world as we know it today.

We have seen how a materialist perspective arose, in part in opposition to theological explanations, and engendered a commitment to human unity. Although there have been times at which alleged biological and more recently cultural discontinuities have been used to explain persistent and historical differences, the mainstream basis of social evolution continues to be materialist. With the demise of idealist and racial explanations and unilinear evolutionism, social evolutionists perforce had to argue that despite generally cross-culturally applicable processes, the historical outcomes ('societies') could not always be the same. They have tended to place the site of difference not so much in prior histories – contingent descent with modification – but in the natural environment or biological processes. Similarly the meaning of social evolution is found in the consequent structural, not 'cultural', organisation of societies. The environment can be construed – as it was by Spencer (and cf. Carneiro 1970) – to encompass the social and political, as well as the physical and ecological.

Nevertheless, explanations for social evolutionary change have tended to reduce to one prime mover: that of population pressure. Given variable environmental conditions, and in conjunction with diffusion, demographic increases supply the motor for intensification and technological change. There are other grounding assumptions about socio-biological behaviour: self-interest, and modern economic rationality drive actual or potential conflict, meaningful differential achievement, social stratification, and the requirement for social integration and leadership. Although the explanations have become more sophisticated, and the database much richer, many of these concepts show extraordinary long-term continuity. With social evolution, not only do the narratives remain similar, but the causal mechanisms also stay largely the same.

This is not to say that progressive social evolution is thereby inevitably tainted by association, but it should perhaps warn us to be particularly careful about its categories and methods. Universal philosophies of history are ultimately based on perceptions about human nature and abilities and the degree to which these characteristics are shared. These have thus been culturally, psychologically, sociologically, biologically, racially and theologically defined. In turn such standpoints determine whether we believe ourselves to be condemned to contingency, able to make our own histories, primarily subject to sociological or even biological laws, or part of a larger cosmic process or vision. This does not make social evolution false as suggested by Tilley (1996: 1) when he suggests that 'grand evolutionary theories positing stages or general processes of world development have proved to be blind alleys'. While such theories ultimately do depend upon cross-cultural (or rather, pan-human) characteristics, politically and intellectually these latter can be used to ascribe rights and moral and ethical duties to all of us, and demand that we treat all people, present and past, with the respect they deserve. They can equally well be used to deny difference and make everyone like us. Similarly difference, as an insistence on irreducible and incommensurable specificities, may be used to justify or deny inequalities. Mary Midgley, discussing 'evolution as a religion' noted that 'facts will never appear to us as brute or meaningless; they will always organise themselves into some sort of story, some drama. These dramas can indeed be dangerous. They can distort our theories, and they have distorted the theory of evolution perhaps more than any other'. However, she continued: 'The only way in which we can control this kind of distortion is, I believe, to bring the dramas themselves out into the open, to give them our full attention, understand them better and see what part, if any, each of them ought to play both in theory and in life' (Midgley 2002: 4). None of us who thinks about the past can remain neutral on these issues – rejection or acceptance of the premises and narratives of progressive or regressive social evolution is just as telling. Defining where we stand in relation to social evolutionary views is part of a much larger debate about what we are, and where we go from here.

Bibliography

Andreski, S., 1969, 'Introduction', in H. Spencer *Principles of Sociology*, ed. and abridged S. Andreski. London: ix-xxxvi.

Andreski, S. (ed.), 1971, *Herbert Spencer: Structure, Function and Evolution*. London.

Appleby, J., 1978, *Economic Thought and Ideology in Seventeenth-Century England*. Princeton.

Arias, P., 1999, 'The origins of the Neolithic along the Atlantic coast of continental Europe: a survey', *Journal of World Prehistory* 13: 403-64.

Armit, I., & W. Finlayson, 1992, 'Hunter-gatherers transformed: the transition to agriculture in northern and western Europe', *Antiquity* 66: 664-76.

Barnard, A., 1983, 'Contemporary hunter-gatherers: current theoretical issues in ecology and social organization', *Annual Review of Anthropology* 12: 193-214.

Barnard, A., 1999, 'Images of hunters and gatherers in European social thought', in *The Cambridge Encyclopedia of Hunters and Gatherers*, eds R. Lee & R. Daly. Cambridge: 375-83.

Barnard, A., 2004, 'Hunter-gatherers in history, archaeology and anthropology: introductory essay', in *Hunter-gatherers in History, Archaeology and Anthropology*, ed. A. Barnard. Oxford: 8-23.

Bender, B., 1978, 'Gatherer-hunter to farmer: a social perspective', *World Archaeology* 10(2): 204-22.

Bender, B., 1989, 'The roots of inequality', in *Domination and Resistance*, eds D. Miller, M. Rowlands & C. Tilley. London: 83-95.

Bender, B. & B. Morris, 1988, 'Twenty years of history, evolution and social change in gatherer-hunter studies', in *Hunters and Gatherers 1: History, Evolution and Social Change*, eds T. Ingold, D. Riches & J. Woodburn. Oxford: 4-14.

Benedict, R., 1935, *Patterns of Culture*. London.

Bibliography

Berkhofer, R., 1978, *The White Man's Indian. Images of the American Indian from Columbus to the Present.* New York.

Bieder, R., 1986, *Science Encounters the Indian, 1820-1880. The Early Years of American Ethnology.* Norman.

Bird-David, N., 1994, 'Sociality and immediacy: or, past and present conversations on bands', *Man* (n.s.) 29: 583-603.

Black, A., 1989, *Man and Nature in the Philosophical Thought of Wang Fu-chih.* Seattle.

Boas, F., 1896, 'The limitations of the comparative method of anthropology', *Science* 4: 901-8.

Boas, F., 1974a [1904], 'The history of anthropology', in *Readings in the History of Anthropology*, ed. R. Degnell. New York: 260-73.

Boas, F., 1974b [1908], 'Anthropology: A Lecture Delivered at Columbia University in the Series on Science, Philosophy, and Art, December 18, 1907', in *The Shaping of American Anthropology 1883-1911: A Franz Boas Reader*, ed. G. Stocking. New York: 267-81.

Bodde, D., 1981, 'Harmony and conflict in Chinese philosophy', in *Essays on Chinese Civilization*, eds C. Le Blanc & D. Borei. Princeton, NJ: 237-98.

Bogucki, P., 2000, 'How agriculture came to north-central Europe', in *Europe's First Farmers*, ed. T. Price. Cambridge: 197-218.

Bowler, P., 1989, *The Invention of Progress: The Victorians and the Past.* Oxford.

Boyd, R. & P. Richerson, 1985, *Culture and the Evolutionary Process.* Chicago.

Braidwood, R., 1981, 'Archaeological retrospect 2', *Antiquity* 55: 19-26.

Brown, D., 1972, *Bury My Heart at Wounded Knee: An Indian History of the American West.* New York.

Burrow, J., 1966, *Evolution and Society: A Study in Victorian Social Theory.* Cambridge.

Carneiro, R., 1970, 'A theory of the origin of the state', *Science* 169: 733-8.

Carneiro, R., 1987, 'Cross-currents in the theory of state formation', *American Ethnologist* 14: 756-70.

Carneiro, R., 2003, *Evolutionism in Cultural Anthropology: A Critical History.* Boulder, Co.

Carson, R., 1962, *Silent Spring.* Boston.

Chapman, R., 2003, *Archaeologies of Complexity.* London.

Chazan, M., 1995, 'Conceptions of time and the development of Paleolithic chronology', *American Anthropologist* 97: 457-67.

Bibliography

Cherry, J., 1978, 'Generalization and the archaeology of the State', in *Social Organisation and Settlement, Part ii* (BAR International Series 47), eds D. Green, C. Haselgrove & M. Spriggs. Oxford: 411-37.

Childe, V.G., 1935, 'Changing methods and aims in prehistory: presidential address for 1935', *Proceedings of the Prehistoric Society* 1: 1-15.

Childe, V.G., 1936, *Man Makes Himself.* London.

Childe, V.G., 1951, *Social Evolution.* London.

Childe, V.G., 1964 [1942], *What Happened in History.* Harmondsworth.

Clark, G., 1980, *Mesolithic Prelude.* Edinburgh.

Clarke, D., 1973, 'Archaeology: the loss of innocence', *Antiquity* 47: 6-18.

Cohen, M., 1977, *The Food Crisis in Prehistory: Overpopulation and the Origins of Agriculture.* New Haven.

Cosgrove, D., 1993, 'Landscapes and myths, gods and humans', in *Landscape: Politics and Perspectives*, ed. B. Bender. Oxford: 281-305.

Daniel, G., 1964, *The Idea of Prehistory.* Harmondsworth.

Dawkins, B., 1894, 'On the relation of the Palaeolithic to the Neolithic period', *Journal of the Royal Anthropological Institute* (o s) 23: 242-57.

Degler, C., 1991, *In Search of Human Nature: The Decline and Revival of Darwinism in American Social Thought.* New York.

Diamond, S., 1974, *In Search of the Primitive: A Critique of Civilization.* New Brunswick.

Diodorus Siculus, 1933, *Diodorus of Sicily (Books I and II)*, tr. C. Oldfather. London.

Dobres, M.-A., and J. Robb (eds), 2000, *Agency in Archaeology.* London.

Dumont, L., 1977, *From Mandeville to Marx. The Genesis and Triumph of Economic Ideology.* Chicago.

Dumont, P.-E., 1965, 'Primitivism in Indian literature', in *Primitivism and Related Ideas in Antiquity*, eds A. Lovejoy & G. Boas. New York: 433-46.

Ehrlich, P., 1968, *The Population Bomb.* New York.

Eliade, M., 1991 [1949], *The Myth of the Eternal Return, or, Cosmos and History.* Princeton, N.J.

Fabian, J., 1983, *Time and the Other: How Anthropology Makes its Object.* New York.

139

Bibliography

Ferguson, A., 1993, *Utter Antiquity. Perceptions of Prehistory in Renaissance England*. Durham, NC.

Flannery, K., 1999, 'Process and agency in early state formation', *Cambridge Archaeological Journal* 9: 3-21.

Fontenelle, B. le Bovier de, 1708, *Fontenelle's Dialogues of the Dead: in Three Parts. I. Dialogues of the Antients. II. The Antients with the Moderns. III. The Moderns; with a Reply to Some Remarks in a Critique, Call'd The Judgement of Pluto, &c. and Two Original Dialogues*. London.

Forster, M., 2001, 'Johann Gottfried von Herder', in *The Stanford Encyclopedia of Philosophy* (Winter 2001 edition), ed. E. Zalta: http://plato.stanford.edu/archives/win2001/entries/herder/

Fried, M., 1967, *The Evolution of Political Society: An Essay in Political Anthropology*. New York.

Gamble, C., 1992, 'Uttermost ends of the earth', *Antiquity* 66: 710-20.

Gates, P., 1971, 'Indian allotments preceding the Dawes Act', in *The Frontier Challenge: Responses to the Trans-Mississippi West*, ed. J. Clark. Lawrence: 141-70.

Gebauer, A. & T. Price, 1992, 'Foragers to farmers: an introduction', in *Transitions to Agriculture in Prehistory (Monographs in World Archaeology 4)*, eds A. Gebauer & T. Price. Madison: 1-10.

Gell, A., 1992, *The Anthropology of Time: Cultural Constructions of Temporal Maps and Images*. Oxford.

Glacken, C., 1967, *Traces on the Rhodian Shore: Nature and Culture in Western Thought from Ancient Times to the End of the Eighteenth Century*. Berkeley.

Goguet, A.-Y., 1761, *The Origin of Laws, Art, Sciences, and their Progress among the most ancient Nations*. Edinburgh.

Halbfass, W., 1988, *India and Europe: An Essay in Understanding*. Albany.

Hallpike, C., 1988, *The Principles of Social Evolution*. Oxford.

Harlan, J., 1995, *The Living Fields: Our Agricultural Heritage*. Cambridge.

Harris, M., 1977, *Cannibals and Kings: The Origins of Cultures*. New York.

Harris, M., 1979, *Cultural Materialism: The Struggle for a Science of Culture*. New York.

Harris, M., 2001, *The Rise of Anthropological Theory: A History of Theories of Culture* (revised edition). Walnut Creek.

Hegel, G., 1956, *The Philosophy of History*, tr. J. Sibree. New York.

Bibliography

Herder, J., 1968, *Reflections on the Philosophy of the History of Mankind*, tr. T. Churchill, ed. F. Manuel. Chicago.

Hodder, I., 1990, *The Domestication of Europe*. Oxford.

Hodgen, M., 1964, *Early Anthropology in the Sixteenth and Seventeenth Centuries*. Philadelphia.

Hofstadter, R., 1992, *Social Darwinism in American Thought*. Boston.

Horsman, R., 1968, 'American Indian policy and the origins of Manifest Destiny', *University of Birmingham Historical Journal* 11: 128-40.

Horsman, R., 1975, 'Scientific racism and the American Indian in the mid-nineteenth century', *American Quarterly* 27: 152-68.

Huntington, S., 1996, *The Clash of Civilizations and the Remaking of World Order* New York.

Ingold, T., 1986, *Evolution and Social Life*. Cambridge.

Jahoda, G., 1999, *Images of Savages. Ancient Roots of Modern Prejudice in Western Culture*. London.

Janko, J., 1997, 'Two concepts of the world in Greek and Roman thought: cyclicity and degeneration', in *Nature and Society in Historical Context*, eds M. Teich, R. Porter & B. Gustaffson. Cambridge: 18-36.

Johnson, A. & T. Earle, 1987, *The Evolution of Human Societies: From Foraging Group to Agrarian State*. Stanford.

Johnson, A. & T. Earle, 2000, *The Evolution of Human Societies: From Foraging Group to Agrarian State* (2nd edition). Stanford.

Kames, Lord (Henry Home), 1774, *Sketches of the History of Man*. Edinburgh.

Kaplan, D., 1960, 'The Law of Cultural Dominance', in *Evolution and Culture*, eds M. Sahlins & E. Service. Ann Arbor: 69-92.

Keech McIntosh, S., 1999, *Beyond Chiefdoms: Pathways to Complexity in Africa*. Cambridge.

Keegan, J., 2001, 'In this war of civilisations, the West will prevail', *The Daily Telegraph* 8 October.
http://www.dailytelegraph.com/opinion.

Kehoe, A., 1998, *The Land of Prehistory: A Critical History of American Archaeology*. New York.

Kintz, T., 2001, 'Archaeologists as intellectuals: agents of the empire or defenders of dissent?', in *The Responsibilities of Archaeologists: Archaeology and Ethics* (BAR International Series 981), ed. M. Pluciennik. Oxford: 47-55.

Klindt-Jensen, O., 1975, *A History of Scandinavian Archaeology*. London.

Bibliography

Kotsakis, K., 2002, 'Review of Catherine Perlès, *The Early Neolithic in Greece*', *European Journal of Archaeology* 5: 373-7.

Kroeber, A., 1923, *Anthropology*. New York.

Kropotkin, P., 1902, *Mutual Aid: A Factor of Evolution*. Boston.

Kuklick, H., 1997, 'After Ishmael: the fieldwork tradition and its future', in *Anthropological Locations. Boundaries and Grounds of a Field Science*, eds A. Gupta & A. Ferguson. Berkeley: 47-65.

Kuper, A., 1996, *Anthropology and Anthropologists: The Modern British School* (3rd edition). London.

Laufer, B., 1918, 'Review of *Culture and Ethnology* by Robert H. Lowie', *American Anthropologist* 20: 87-91.

Layton, R., 1989, 'Introduction: who needs the past?', in *Who Needs the Past? Indigenous Values and Archaeology*, ed. R. Layton. London: 1-20.

Leacock, E. & R. Lee (eds), 1982, *Politics and History in Band Societies*. Cambridge.

Lee, R., 1979, *The !Kung San: Men, Women and Work in a Foraging Society*. Cambridge.

Lee, R. & R. Daly, 1999, 'Introduction: foragers and others', in *The Cambridge Encyclopedia of Hunters and Gatherers*, eds R. Lee and R. Daly. Cambridge: 1-19.

Leopold, J., 1980, *Culture in Comparative and Evolutionary Perspective: E.B. Tylor and the Making of Primitive Culture*. Berlin.

Lesser, A., 1985, 'Evolution in social anthropology', in *History, Evolution, and the Concept of Culture: Selected Papers by Alexander Lesser*, ed. S. Mintz. Cambridge: 78-91.

Lovejoy, A. & G. Boas, 1965, *Primitivism and Related Ideas in Antiquity*. New York.

Lowie, R., 1949 [1920], *Primitive Society*. London.

Lubbock, J., 1870, *The Origins of Civilisation and the Primitive Condition of Man: Mental and Social Condition of Savages* (2nd edition). London.

MacCormack, C., 1980, 'Nature, culture and gender: a critique', in *Nature, Culture and Gender*, eds C. MacCormack & M. Strathern. Cambridge: 1-24.

McGrane, B., 1989, *Beyond Anthropology: Society and the Other*. New York.

McLennan, J., 1869, 'The early history of man', *North British Review* (o.s.) 50: 516-49.

Malik, K., 2000, *Man, Beast and Zombie: What Science Can and Cannot Tell Us About Human Nature*. London.

Mandelbaum, M., 1971, *History, Man, and Reason: A Study in Nineteenth-Century Thought*. Baltimore.

Mandeville, B., 1970 [1724], *The Fable of the Bees*, ed. P. Harth. Harmondsworth.

Massey, D., 1999, 'Space-time, "science" and the relationship between physical geography and human geography', *Transactions of the Institute of British Geographers* (n.s.) 24: 261-76.

Mazurié de Keroualin, K., 2003, *Genèse et Diffusion de l'Agriculture en Europe: Agriculteurs-Chasseurs-Pasteurs*. Paris.

Mead, M., 1942 [1930], *Growing Up in New Guinea*. Harmondsworth.

Mead, M., 1943 [1928], *Coming of Age in Samoa*. Harmondsworth.

Meek, R., 1976, *Social Science and the Ignoble Savage*. Cambridge.

Midgley, M., 2002, *Evolution as a Religion: Strange Hopes and Stranger Fears* (revised edition). London.

Mill, J.S., 1974, *On Liberty*, ed. G. Himmelfarb. Harmondsworth.

Mink, L., 1981, 'Everyman his or her own Annalist', *Critical Inquiry* 7: 777-83.

Montesquieu, [Charles de Secondat], Baron de, 1989, *The Spirit of the Laws*, tr. and ed. A. Cohler, B. Miller & H. Stone. Cambridge.

Morgan. L., 1877, *Ancient Society, or, Researches in the Lines of Human Progress from Savagery through Barbarism to Civilization*. New York.

Murdock, G., 1934, *Our Primitive Contemporaries*. New York.

Needham, J., 1965, *Time and Eastern Man (Royal Anthropological Institute Occasional Paper 21)*. London.

Nisbet, R., 1980, *History of the Idea of Progress*. London.

Paddaya, K., 1995, 'Theoretical perspectives in Indian archaeology', in *Theory in Archaeology: a World Perspective*, ed. P. Ucko. London: 110-49.

Pagden, A., 1986, *The Fall of Natural Man. The American Indian and the Origins of Comparative Ethnology*. Cambridge.

Pagden, A., 1993, *European Encounters with the New World: From Renaissance to Romanticism*. New Haven.

Patterson, T., 1997, *Inventing Western Civilization*. New York.

Patterson, T., 2001, *A Social History of Anthropology in the United States*. Oxford.

Peake, H., 1927, 'The beginning of civilization', *Journal of the Royal Anthropological Institute* (o.s.) 57: 19-38.

Perlès, C., 2001, *The Early Neolithic in Greece: The First Farming Communities in Europe*. Cambridge.

Bibliography

Perrault, C., 1964 [1688-1697], *Parallèle des Anciens et des Modernes en ce qui Regarde les Arts et les Sciences*. München.

Pluciennik, M., 1997, 'Radiocarbon determinations and the mesolithic-neolithic transition in southern Italy', *Journal of Mediterranean Archaeology* 10: 115-50.

Pluciennik, M., 1998, 'Deconstructing "the neolithic" in the mesolithic-neolithic transition', in *Understanding the Neolithic of North-Western Europe*, eds M. Edmonds & C. Richards. Glasgow: 61-83.

Pluciennik, M., 1999, 'Archaeological narratives and other ways of telling', *Current Anthropology* 40: 653-78.

Pluciennik, M., 2002, 'The invention of hunter-gatherers in seventeenth-century Europe', *Archaeological Dialogues* 9(2): 98-151.

Pluciennik, M., 2004, 'The meaning of "hunter-gatherers" and modes of subsistence: a comparative historical perspective', in *Hunter-gatherers in History, Archaeology and Anthropology*, ed. A. Barnard. Oxford: 25-41.

Pluciennik, M. and M. Zvelebil, 2003, 'Historical origins of agriculture', in *The Role of Food, Agriculture, Forestry and Fisheries in Human Nutrition*, ed. V. Squires, *Encyclopedia of Food and Agricultural Sciences, Engineering and Technology Resources*. Online Encyclopedia of Life Support Systems. Oxford: http://www.eolss.net/

Popkin, R., 1973, 'The philosophical basis of eighteenth-century racism', *Studies in Eighteenth Century History* 3: 245-62.

Porter, R., 1979, 'Creation and credence: the career of theories of the earth in Britain, 1660-1820', in *Natural Order: Historical Studies of Scientific Culture*, eds B. Barnes & S. Shapin. Beverly Hills: 97-123.

Price, T., 2000, 'Europe's first farmers: an introduction', in *Europe's First Farmers*, ed. T. Price. Cambridge: 1-18.

Price, T. & J. Brown (eds), 1985, *Prehistoric Hunter-Gatherers: The Emergence of Cultural Complexity*. Orlando.

Prucha, F., 1969, 'Andrew Jackson's Indian policy: a reassessment', *Journal of American History* 56: 527-39.

Prucha, F., 1971, 'American-Indian policy in the 1840s: visions of reform', in *The Frontier Challenge: Responses to the Trans-Mississipi West*, ed. J. Clark. Lawrence: 81-110.

Quesnay, F. & Mirabeau, Marquis de, 1962, 'Extract from "Rural Philosophy"', in *The Economics of Physiocracy. Essays and Translations*, ed. R. Meek. Cambridge, MA: 57-64.

Bibliography

Redfield, R., 1953, *The Primitive World and its Transformations*. New York.

Renfrew, C., 1973a, *Before Civilisation: The Radiocarbon Revolution and Prehistoric Europe*. London.

Renfrew, C., 1973b, 'Monuments, mobilisation and social organisation in Neolithic Wessex', in *The Explanation of Culture Change: Models in Prehistory*, ed. C. Renfrew. London: 539-58.

Renfrew, C. & J. Cherry (eds), 1986, *Peer Polity Interaction and Socio-Political Change*. Cambridge.

Resek, C., 1960, *Lewis Henry Morgan: American Scholar*. Chicago.

Rindos, D., 1984, *The Origin of Agricultural Systems: An Evolutionary Perspective*. New York.

Robertson, W., 1783 [1777], *The History of America* (4th edition). Edinburgh.

Rodden, J., 1981, 'The development of the Three Age system: archaeology's first paradigm', in *Towards a History of Archaeology*, ed. G. Daniel. London: 51-68.

Rowlands, M., 1989, 'A question of complexity', in *Domination and Resistance*, eds D. Miller, M. Rowlands & C. Tilley. London: 29-40.

Rowley-Conwy, P., 2001, 'Time, change and the archaeology of hunter-gatherers: how original is the "Original Affluent Society"?', in *Hunter-Gatherers: An Interdisciplinary Perspective*, eds C. Panter-Brick, R. Layton & P. Rowley-Conwy. Cambridge: 39-72.

Rudebeck, E., 2000, *Tilling Nature, Harvesting Culture: Exploring Images of the Human Being in the Transition to Agriculture* (Acta Archaeologica Lundensia, 8th Series, 32). Stockholm.

Sahlins, M., 1960, 'Evolution: specific and general', in *Evolution and Culture*, eds M. Sahlins & E. Service. Ann Arbor: 12-44.

Sahlins, M., 1968, 'Notes on the original affluent society', in *Man the Hunter*, eds R. Lee & I. DeVore. Chicago: 85-9.

Sahlins, M. & E. Service (eds), 1960, *Evolution and Culture*. Ann Arbor.

Said, E., 1978, *Orientalism*. New York.

Sanderson, S., 1990, *Social Evolutionism: A Critical History*. Cambridge MA.

Sanderson, S., 1995, *Social Transformations: A General Theory of Historical Development*. Oxford.

Sanderson, S., 2002, 'How Chase-Dunn and Hall got it almost right. Review of Christopher Chase-Dunn and Thomas D. Hall, *Rise and Demise: Comparing World Systems*', *Social Evolution and History* 1: 171-6.

Bibliography

Schaffer, S., 1997, 'The earth's fertility as a social fact in early modern Britain', in *Nature and Society in Historical Context*, eds M. Teich, R. Porter & B. Gustafsson. Cambridge: 124-47.

Schumacher, E. F., 1973, *Small is Beautiful: A Study of Economics as if People Mattered*. London.

Service, E., 1960, 'The Law of Evolutionary Potential', in *Evolution and Culture*, eds M. Sahlins & E. Service. Ann Arbor: 93-122.

Service, E., 1971 [1962], *Primitive Social Organization: An Evolutionary Perspective* (2nd edition). New York.

Shennan, S., 1993, 'After social evolution: a new archaeological agenda?', in *Archaeological Theory: Who Sets the Agenda?* eds N. Yoffee & A. Sherratt. Cambridge: 53-9.

Shennan, S., 2002, *Genes, Memes and Human History: Darwinian Archaeology and Cultural Evolution*. London.

Silverberg, R., 1968, *Mound Builders of Ancient America. The Archaeology of a Myth*. Greenwich, Conn.

Simmons, I., 1996, *The Environmental Impact of Later Mesolithic Cultures*. Edinburgh.

Skeates, R., 2003, 'Radiocarbon dating and interpretations of the Mesolithic-Neolithic transition in Italy', in *The Widening Harvest. The Neolithic Transition in Europe: Looking Back, Looking Forward*, eds A. Ammerman & P. Biagi. Boston, MA: 157-87.

Slotkin, J. (ed.), 1965, *Readings in Early Anthropology*. London.

Smith, A., 1970 [1776], *The Wealth of Nations*. Harmondsworth.

Smith, A.T., 2003, *The Political Landscape: Constellations of Authority in Early Complex Polities*. Berkeley.

Smith, B., 1994, *The Emergence of Agriculture*. New York.

Smith, G., 1916, 'Primitive Man', *Proceedings of the British Academy 1915-1916*: 455-504.

Sollas, W., 1911, *Ancient Hunters and their Modern Representatives*. London.

Spencer, H., 1969, *Principles of Sociology*, ed. and abridged S. Andreski. London.

Steward, J., 1949, 'Cultural causality and law: a trial formulation of the development of early civilizations', *American Anthropologist* 51: 1-27.

Steward, J., 1955a, 'The concept and method of cultural ecology', in *Theory of Culture Change: The Methodology of Multilinear Evolution*. Urbana: 30-42.

Steward, J., 1955b [1952], 'Multilinear evolution: evolution and process', in *Theory of Culture Change: The Methodology of Multilinear Evolution.* Urbana: 11-29.

Steward, J., 1955c, 'Introduction' in *Theory of Culture Change: The Methodology of Multilinear Evolution.* Urbana: 3-8.

Stocking, G., 1982, 'The persistence of polygenist thought in post-Darwinian anthropology', in *Race, Culture, and Evolution.* Chicago: 42-68.

Stocking, G., 1987, *Victorian Anthropology.* New York.

Stocking, G., 1996, *After Tylor: British Social Anthropology 1888-1951.* London.

Stoczkowski, W., 2002, *Explaining Human Origins: Myth, Imagination and Conjecture,* tr. M. Turton. Cambridge.

Tainter, J., 1988, *The Collapse of Complex Societies.* Cambridge.

Thomas, J., 1993, 'Discourse, totalization and "The Neolithic" ', in *Interpretative Archaeology,* ed. C. Tilley. Providence: 357-94.

Thomas, J., 1996, 'The cultural context of the first use of domesticates in continental central and northwest Europe', in *The Origin and Spread of Agriculture and Pastoralism in Eurasia,* ed. D. Harris. London: 310-22.

Tilley, C., 1995, 'Clowns and circus acts: a response to Trigger', *Critique of Anthropology* 15: 337-41.

Tilley, C., 1996, *An Ethnography of the Neolithic: Early Prehistoric Societies in Southern Scandinavia.* Cambridge.

Trautmann, T., 1992, 'The revolution in ethnological time', *Man* (n.s.) 27: 379-97.

Trigger, B., 1989, *A History of Archaeological Thought.* Cambridge.

Trigger, B., 1995, 'Archaeology and the integrated circus', *Critique of Anthropology* 15: 319-35.

Trigger, B., 1998, *Sociocultural Evolution.* Oxford.

Tringham, R., 2000, 'Southeastern Europe in the transition to agriculture in Europe: bridge, buffer, or mosaic', in *Europe's First Farmers,* ed. T. Price. Cambridge: 19-56.

Turner, F., 1962 [1893], 'The significance of the frontier in American history', in *The Frontier in American History.* New York: 1-38.

Tylor, E., 1865, *Researches into the Early History of Mankind and the Development of Civilization.* London.

Tylor, E. 1871 *Primitive Culture: Researches in the Development of Mythology, Philosophy, Religion, Art, and Custom* (2 vols). London.

Tylor, E., 1881, *Anthropology: An Introduction to the Study of Man and Civilization.* London.

Voget, F., 1967, 'Progress, science, history and evolution in eighteenth-

Bibliography

and nineteenth-century anthropology', *Journal of the History of the Behavioural Sciences* 3: 132-55.

Wallerstein, I., 1983, *Historical Capitalism*. London.

Warder, A., 1961, 'The Pali Canon and its commentaries as an historical record', in *Historians of India, Pakistan and Ceylon*, ed. C. Philips. London: 44-56.

White, H., 1973, *Metahistory: The Historical Imagination in Nineteenth-Century Europe*. Baltimore.

White, H., 1981, 'The narrativization of real events', *Critical Inquiry* 7: 793-8.

White, H., 1987, *The Content of the Form: Narrative Discourse and Historical Representation*. Baltimore.

White, L., 1938, 'Science is sciencing', *Philosophy of Science* 5: 369-89.

White, L., 1945, 'History, evolutionism, and functionalism: three types of interpretation of culture', *Southwest Journal of Anthropology* 1: 221-48.

White, L., 1949a, 'Energy and the evolution of culture', in *The Science of Culture: A Study of Man and Civilization*. New York: 263-393.

White, L., 1949b (1947], 'The expansion of the scope of science', in *The Science of Culture: A Study of Man and Civilization*. New York: 55-117.

White, L., 1949c, 'The science of culture', in *The Science of Culture: A Study of Man and Civilization*. New York: 397-415.

White, L., 1959, *The Evolution of Culture: The Development of Civilization to the Fall of Rome*. New York

White, L., 1987, *Leslie A. White: Ethnological Essays*, eds B. Dillingham & R. Carneiro. Albuquerque.

Whittle, A., 1996, *Europe in the Neolithic: The Creation of New Worlds*. Cambridge.

Willey, G. & J. Sabloff, 1974, *A History of American Archaeology*. San Francisco.

Williams, R., 1975, *The Country and the City*. Frogmore.

Wittfogel, K., 1957, *Oriental Despotism: A Comparative Study of Total Power*. New Haven.

Wolf, E., 1982, *Europe and the People without History*. Berkeley.

Woodburn, J., 1980, 'Hunters and gatherers today and reconstruction of the past', in *Soviet and Western Anthropology*, ed. E. Gellner. London: 95-117.

Wylie, A., 1989, 'Archaeological cables and tacking: the implications of practice for Bernstein's "Options beyond objectivism and relativism" ', *Philosophy of the Social Sciences* 19: 1-18.

Bibliography

Yoffee, N., 1993, 'Too many chiefs? (Or, safe texts for the '90s)', in *Archaeological Theory: Who Sets the Agenda?* eds N. Yoffee & A. Sherratt. Cambridge: 60-78.

Zvelebil, M. 1996a, 'The agricultural frontier and the transition to farming in the circum-Baltic region', in *The Origins and Spread of Agriculture and Pastoralism in Eurasia*, ed. D. Harris. London: 323-45.

Zvelebil, M., 1996b, 'Farmers our ancestors and the identity of Europe', in *Cultural Identity and Archaeology: The Construction of European Communities*, eds P. Graves-Brown, S. Jones & C. Gamble. London: 145-66.

Zvelebil, M., 1997, 'Hunter-gatherer ritual landscapes: spatial organisation, social structure and ideology among hunter-gatherers of northern Europe and western Siberia', *Analecta Praehistorica Leidensia* 29: 33-50.

Zvelebil, M., 1998, 'Agricultural frontiers, Neolithic origins, and the transition to farming in the Baltic basin', in *Harvesting the Sea, Farming the Forest: The Emergence of Neolithic Societies in the Baltic Region*, eds M. Zvelebil, L. Domanska & R. Dennell. Sheffield: 9-27.

Zvelebil, M., L. Domanska & R. Dennell, 1998, 'Introduction: The Baltic and the transition to farming', in *Harvesting the Sea, Farming the Forest: The Emergence of Neolithic Societies in the Baltic Region*, eds M. Zvelebil, L. Domanska and R. Dennell. Sheffield: 1-7.

Index

Index

153

p 79 coolution as prove to 'light' down?
p 89 „ ☰ progress